STRATEGIC FINANCE
Achieving High Corporate Performance

ALNOOR BHIMANI

Strategy Press
19 Carlton Avenue
London, U.K.
N14 4TY
www. Strategypress.com

© Alnoor Bhimani, 2013

The rights of Alnoor Bhimani to be identified as author of this work have been asserted by him in accordance with the Copyright, Designs and Patents Act 1988.

All rights reserved. No part of this publication may be reproduced, stored in a retrieval system, or transmitted in any form or by any means, electronic, mechanical, photocopying, recording or otherwise without the prior written permission of the publisher

ISBN   978-09541477-3-0

TABLE OF CONTENTS

PREFACE

1 **BUSINESS IN A WORLD OF**   1
   EXTREME CHANGE
The New Business Order
How unique should Strategic Finance be?
Strategic Finance in Action
Yesterday's Strategy – Tomorrow's Commodity
What Strategic Finance can Achieve

2 **PROFIT AND RISK**   20
Costing Things
Costs and Expenses
The Components of Product Costs
Reflections on Cost Behaviour
Intelligent Regression
Achieving profitability
Examples of CVP in action
Contribution Margin Analysis
Standards for Managing Risks
Standard Costing and Variance Analysis

3 **FROM FLEXIBLE TO FLUID ORGANIZATIONS**   48
Technological Change and Cost Management
    The 'New' Economics of Cost Management
Quality: What is it and How Much is Enough?
Customers and Quality
Making Cost of Quality Work
Just-in-Time
    Just-In-Case or Just in Time?
Blackflush Accounting
Enterprise Resource Planning
    Do ERP Systems Perform?
Automation and Flexibility

        Computer-Aided Design and Computer-Aided
          Manufacturing
        Flexible and Computer-Integrated Manufacturing
          Systems
    Additive Manufacturing
    Creating Fluid Organizations

4   **MAKING ACTIVITIES PROFITABLE**   98
    Changing Standards
    The ABC Phenomenon
    What Drives Costs?
    The Logic Of Activity Analysis
    Scope versus Scale
        Long-term versus Short-term Cost Behaviour
    What is an Activity?
    When To Replace A Costing System
    System Design Issues
    Economic Logic and Organizational Realities

5   **MEASURES THAT PERFORM**   125
    The Goals of Performance Measures
    Designing Effective Performance Measurement Systems
    Why New Performance Measures?
    In Search of Balance
    The Balanced Scorecard
    The Balanced Scorecard and Strategy
    The Effective Implementation of a Balanced Scorecard
    Balanced Scorecards Can Fail!
    The Balanced Scorecard and Risk Management

6   **STRATEGY MATTERS**   153
    Strategy and Planning
    Competitive Differentiation
    Competitive Forces
    Core Competencies
    Why Do Strategies Fail?
    Strategic Controls
    Strategic Control Criteria
    Implementing issues
    Strategic Cost Analysis: Tying Value to Costs

Analyzing Customer Profitability
Strategy and Customer Profitability Analysis

7 **TIMING, MARKET AND STRATEGIC ISSUES** 190
Time and Product Life Cycles
Strategy and Target Cost Management
Putting Target Costing Principles Into Effect
Strategic Synergy in Action

8 **FINANCIAL MANAGEMENT AND DIGITIZATION** 209
Digitization and Disruption
Levels of Impact
  Managerial Concerns
  Strategy
  Pricing
  Quality
Organizational Issues
  Standardizing Financial Management Systems
Macro-Shifts: Data, Information and Knowledge
Transparency in an 'E-world'

BIBLIOGRAPHY 233

PREFACE

In making day-to-day operational or wider impact strategic decisions, executives need to analyze financial, managerial and market based information. Such analysis is at the heart of strategic finance. This book explains how strategic finance can help bring about high operational and strategic performance in modern enterprises. In times of both economic boom and downturn, financial information needs to be coupled with customer and market knowledge to make visible profitable opportunities. The 'new' normal environment within which executives operate today is one of extreme uncertainty. Strategic finance assists enterprises not just to deal with conditions of high risk and uncertainty but to drive change as part of their competitive strategy.

The aim of this book is to equip you with the capacity to make decisions that are grounded in an understanding of financial information and market-based business intelligence and to enable you to drive managerial and strategic engagement that maximizes value creation. The book is highly practical ensuring immediate applicability in enterprises. Some of the broad areas discussed include:

- The speed of business change confronting managers
- The impact of flexible and digital technologies
- Managerial accounting and marketing issues
- E-business pursuits and financial management techniques
- The links between enterprise structures and rewards
- The challenges of shortening product and life-cycles
- The outsourcing of support and core enterprise functions
- Organizational culture issues in financial control
- Customer information as a source of managerial insight
- Time-based financial information

- Strategy and digitization
- Business analytics and non-economic data intelligence
- Risk and governance

The book makes transparent how strategy, finance and other management functions interface. It explains with high clarity and numerous case illustrations a number of technical issues of importance in modern enterprises. It provides many examples of the application of strategic, financial, management accounting and related approaches and concepts with discussions of their impact in enterprises. Some topics covered include:

- Incremental profits from differential costing
- Strategic costing and performance analysis
- Flexible organizational technologies and corporate strategy
- Activity based management and profit creation
- Product life-cycle and financial intelligence
- Quality costing
- Customer profitability analysis
- Profit driven risk management
- Target costing and financial control
- Performance management and the balanced scorecard
- E-costing and digital economy issues
- Globalization and strategic finance

The book is aimed at readers who want to understand approaches to strategic management, accounting analysis and financial management and how they can be applied to tackle competitive situations facing managers today. It will prove invaluable to executives and practitioners and students interested in the interconnections between accounting, finance, strategy and modern management.

The book can be read sequentially by those seeking a progressive understanding of the variety of issues facing managers beginning with cost concepts through to strategic and wider enterprise governance insights. Its structure and the links across topics are highlighted in a way that also allows chapters to be read independently of one another. The case illustrations, technical explanations and management focused discussions of issues make evident the great potential of strategic finance for modern firms with high performance expectations and organizational excellence targets.

Alnoor Bhimani
London School of Economics

ABOUT THE AUTHOR

Alnoor Bhimani is Professor of Management Accounting at the London School of Economics where he has previously headed the Department of Accounting. He has studied practices in a variety of global enterprises and has presented his ideas to corporate executives and academic audiences in Europe, Asia, Africa and the Americas. Alnoor is a distinguished scholar known for examining issues of managerial practice and financial leadership as changes in business models and strategies and wider economic and technological shifts take place. He has published over 100 articles in executive management magazines and academic journals. He has co-authored and edited eighteen books with some of the world's best management thinkers. His publications include bestsellers such as *Contemporary Issues in Management Accounting* (Oxford University Press, 2006), *Management Accounting: Retrospect and Prospect* (Elsevier, 2010), and *Management and Cost Accounting* (Pearson, 2012). He is on the editorial board of top academic journals. Alnoor was a Fulbright Fellow at Cornell University in New York where he obtained an MBA and holds a PhD from the London School of Economics. He also qualified as a Certified Management Accountant (Canada).

1

BUSINESS IN A WORLD OF EXTREME CHANGE

Inditex Group's flagship brand is Zara. It makes close to one million garments a year. Over 6000 Zara stores exist. In 2012 it made profits of €2.36 billion on sales of €15.9 billion – 16% up on the previous year. The company's success runs on integrating manufacturing savvy with information. Designers create about three items a day with the help of sales specialists who dissect sales reports from Zara stores across 80 countries and analyse information on what customers look at. Webcams across global sites act as trendspotters, bloggers are tracked and customers are closely watched for what they purchase and what they don't. A 38000 square metre logistics department delivers customised orders to every Zara store on the planet – within 24 to 48 hour turnaround deadlines. Amancio Ortega, founder of the company and third richest man in the world, has ensured the company is flat structured, makes decisions based on colour, feel of fabric and trend information and by prioritising customer preferences and extreme speed. Strategic, market-based and financial information is core to what has made Zara a spectacular success. Zara has set a new order for business which other clothing retailers have found hard to follow.

The New Business Order

All enterprises are affected by change. The forces of globalisation, financial crises, shifting world demographics and the economic rise of developing nations are reshaping world markets for products and services. New business models are emerging and maturing at previously unimagined speed. Traditional markets and products are being extinguished with new product types and novel production and delivery techniques emerging. A dramatic alteration in the intellectual *landscape* within which enterprises operate has been in evidence in recent years.

Extreme change is an expectation rather than a deviation in the 'new normal' economy we find ourselves in. Many successful enterprises like Zara are seeking to envision ways to create such change to challenge their competition. The search for new drivers of economic performance is a corporate necessity which is redefining the rules of competition.

A key question confronting companies is how to balance the needs of financial stability whilst also assessing opportunities in a way that ensures being able to sustain a profitable and competitive posture. Both financial control and strategic assessment must constantly be carried out by enterprises. Many novel financial control practices have been developed recently to help enterprises perform competitive and strategic analyses and to provide informational and decision making support. Some companies now operate across industries and have multiple corporate objectives with opportunities and risks having to be assessed. Certain companies define their products in ways that differ from what their customers might think. Nokia has recently seen itself as the world's biggest camera company. Likewise, the suggestion is often made that Facebook's product is the customer who creates content whilst Facebook says that via 'Product Managers' it builds products such as 'Home', 'Places', 'Beacon' and 'Graph Search'. New business models create competitiveness and cause market shifts. Determining strategy and understanding product opportunities and impact require financial insight that more and more has to be grounded within a wide diversity of information types.

The finance function in many companies attempts to provide a comprehensive service to help managers achieve high levels of performance through a variety of techniques and to bring strategic strength to those parts of their activities most crucial to attaining organizational excellence and higher performance. The task is multi-disciplinary and blind to traditional boundaries of corporate management activities. No longer can functions within organizations be viewed as solitary. This book is concerned with exposing cutting edge expertise from financial management, marketing, strategy and related areas of management in an integrated manner to address the new competitive context surrounding enterprises.

Traditionally, the principal objective of financial controls was to assist organizations plan their future and to monitor performance to ensure that planned objectives were achieved. The emphasis was on internal processes (see Figure 1.1). Control processes as part of financial management activities were mainly concerned with analysing, investigating and forecasting information of a financial and non-financial nature and particularly with examining deviations from expected performance and the implications of these deviations. Finance based practices in many enterprises today encompass much wider and diverse roles in addition to this focused view. Strategic concerns, enterprise design, issues of globalisation, flexible technologies, e-business activities, management style and organizational culture change are facets of modern managerial concerns which now impact financial management. These activities draw from diverse areas of knowledge including management accounting, financial management and cost management as well as technology, marketing and strategic control. This book discusses their interface under the umbrella label of 'strategic finance'.

How Unique Should Strategic Finance Be?

Strategic finance can be regarded as the dynamic interface between modern financial management, managerial control and strategic management. Perhaps the most managerially grounded notion of financial management is that which comprises management accounting action, thought and practice. The term management accounting has been defined by the UK-based Chartered Institute of Management Accountants (CIMA) as:

> The application of the principles of accounting and financial management to create, protect, preserve and increase value so as to deliver that value to the stakeholders of profit and not-for-profit enterprises, both public and private. Management accounting is an integral part of management, requiring the identification, generation, presentation, interpretation and use of information relevant to:

- formulating business strategy;
- planning and controlling activities;
- efficient resource usage;
- performance improvement and value enhancement;
- safeguarding tangible and intangible assets;
- corporate governance and internal control.

What enables management accounting to remain focused on the specific needs of organizations is that there is no compulsion for it to follow externally defined and standardised principles as is the case with external corporate financial reporting. *Financial* information users are *usually* managers with *organization*-specific decision making needs *so it would not make sense to use a uniform approach to meeting their needs.* This renders the finance function highly diverse across organizations. Strategic finance takes an additional leap by embedding strategic management concerns into applied financial management and control activities within modern firms. Its focus becomes both the enabling of reactive responses as well as the mobilisation of proactive change.

Figure 1.1 Traditional Financial Controls: Inward Outlook

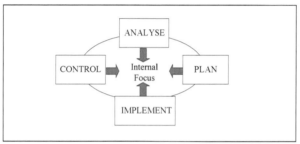

The traditional financial control and management accounting domain has been regarded by some as too narrow and in need of embracing a more operationally engaged role and of possibly providing an advisory service to other parts of enterprises where value can be added. Thus in some firms the finance function has become a consultative business partner, a participant in decision-making and a contributor to more strategically oriented and performance focused activities. Financial expertise tends to spread across management functions because few managers can afford to remain incognizant of the financial context of their decisions and activities.

Table 1.1 The Finance Function: Yesterday and Today

Yesterday	Today
Control is the responsibility of the finance function	Control is the responsibility of every manager and employee. Accounting and finance considerations is everyone's business role is to highlight risk areas and monitor the application of controls
Control is focused on financial accounting and treasury tasks	Financial controls encompass accounting activities, financing performance, risk analysis, business continuity and strategic intelligence
Control checks are applied at the end of discrete business activities (i.e., post-event)	Controls are built into business processes rather than 'added on'. Control is exercised through raising employees' understanding of how they fit in to the organization
Responsibilities are vertically segregated and functions retain independence	Heavy integration of activities require controls to be embedded in business processes horizontally
As control problems become more complex the finance function grows	Managers' needs determine finance function activities. Ultimately customers should not be made to pay for resource usage by the firm which they do not value – including the finance function
The finance function should provide financial and non-financial information for managers to act upon	Managers require the finance function to 'own' decisions. The information form should be limitless encompassing historical and strategic information detailed, aggregated as well as derived from data mining

Finance and management accounting professionals recognize the influencing pressures of various forces on modern enterprises. The need to manage outsourced activities and service centres, to develop new business alliances, to adopt internet-based technologies, and to assess the impact of globalisation has changed the face of what finance executives worry about in recent years. Environmental matters, risk control and the demands of corporate governance where corporate citizenship pressures often exceed strictly legal ones add to their concerns.

The increased demand for information transparency is today evident in a corporate governance intense world and brings with it additional costs. Financial transparency raises costs and raised costs incite the desire for further transparency to promote increased cost containment. Thus at the board level, financial awareness of both operational and strategic action is becoming the norm. Being a non-executive director does not negate the need for both financial understanding and strategic reasoning.

Management and financial control practices within enterprises are in a continual state of adaptation as the knowledge base in the field increases and becomes dispersed and as wider business environment changes take effect. The accounting or finance function is now having to adopt a broader vision of how it can add value to a firm. Many changes in expectations are afoot. What the finance function does, how it shares in decision making, the types of control issues it engages in, the extent to which it delivers financial, non-financial and other types of information including aggregated data mining intelligence are all aspects of its role under revision within different firms (see Table 1.1). Whereas it could be anticipated what a financial manager did in the past across different firms, this is no longer the case today. The finance function of today engages in a panoply of activities *that* differ across organizations. This diversity makes finance organizationally specific. Although some repetitive financial processes are standardised and take place in the same way across different companies, the overall configuration of the finance function and the way it engages with other business functions in a particular enterprise allow it to be a core competitive factor.

Some commentators have advocated a more metric-centric strategic orientation within enterprises. They for instance advocate a quantified formulation and implementation of strategy, to help translate strategic intent and capabilities into operational and managerial measures. Financial management professionals are thought to be in need of moving away from being scorekeepers of the past and to instead become the designers of the organization's critical management information systems (Atkinson et al., 2007). Whilst performance measurement systems seek to focus on improving existing processes, there is in addition, a need to become more 'balanced'. The balanced scorecard (Kaplan and Norton, 2001) focuses on what new processes are needed to achieve breakthrough performance objectives for customers and shareholders.

Understanding the enterprise context is crucial for any financial manager. Today many management accounting techniques and control approaches are used in firms (activity accounting, target costing, the balanced scorecard and strategic cost analysis are examples which are discussed in later sections of the book). The problem is never one of too few solutions being available, but rather of inadequately applied techniques because they are at odds with the realities and uniqueness of organizations and what is essential in their search for particular domains of profitable activity. The adage 'following the crowd does not make you rich' resonates well with the need for any enterprise to contextually determine the essential purpose of its finance function. Standardisation in a technologically savvy and economically complex world does not advance competitive positioning.

In the past, financial managers and management accountants used to focus on how to disclose and report financial accounting numbers and cost information so that managers could draw on them for analysis and decision making. But management accounting systems in some enterprises are now becoming large, real-time databases whereby managers retrieve, manipulate, and analyse new problems as they arise. These firms have opted to implement organization-wide integrated information systems able to capture a vast array of data that they convert into managerially useful information. In complex and fast-changing digital and globalizing markets, the finance professional is called upon to be increasingly integrative and holistic as well as managerial and strategic. This means that non-financial and financial executives both have to interface to assess the business environment and instigate competitive action.

The role of the finance function is moving away from traditional responsibilities into many different areas. Finance executives are expected to be involved in actively formulating business objectives and strategies, enhancing competitive advantage, helping to alter business processes, analysing market trends, implementing quality measurement systems, dealing with governance requirements strategically and delivering value and customer satisfaction like any other operational department.

Strategic Finance In Action

As noted, different organizations address their managerial needs in different ways. Whilst procedures and processes may be alike, interpretations, reliance and actions based on management accounting and financial information generally vary across companies. Finance and accounting-related tasks, responsibilities and pursuits therefore need to be understood in terms of the organizational, cultural and social contexts to which they relate. Enterprises arrange responsibilities for managing organizational resources in different ways. In certain companies, the finance expert's prime interest in financial records is to determine trends in costs, revenues, etc. and deviations from forecasted performance. In other enterprises, the finance function is called upon to provide control support for both operational tasks and strategic management activities. Management accounting and financial control practices in a growing number of organizations are experiencing a transition away from focusing on internal processes and on past priorities toward becoming more externally oriented and managerially implicated. The strategic finance priorities emergent in modern organizations are increasingly a product of the interface between internal and external factors and different sources of information management expertise and concerns (see Figure 1.2).

In looking at the rise of strategic finance activities within enterprises, it is the case that much diversity is in evidence. What constitutes strategic finance is influenced by operational, institutional, cultural and other company-specific factors. A financial manager or a management accountant's role is always influenced by the organizational context. Many external factors affect strategic finance practices as indicated in Figure 1.2. An enterprise's core competence can be the way it structures its financial management activities. For many enterprises today, reams of data emanates from financial transactions, operational movements and customer interactions partly collected from new devices placed throughout multiple points in the value chain. In some companies, sensors embedded in machinery and radio frequency identification based on intelligent bar codes to track items produce cascading information of use to firms. The era of 'big data' made possible through new technologies implies new and expanded data sources. The analysis of macro-volume data can reveal 'order within chaos' and 'hidden trends' which can have significant implications for decision making.

Figure 1.2 Strategic Finance in Action

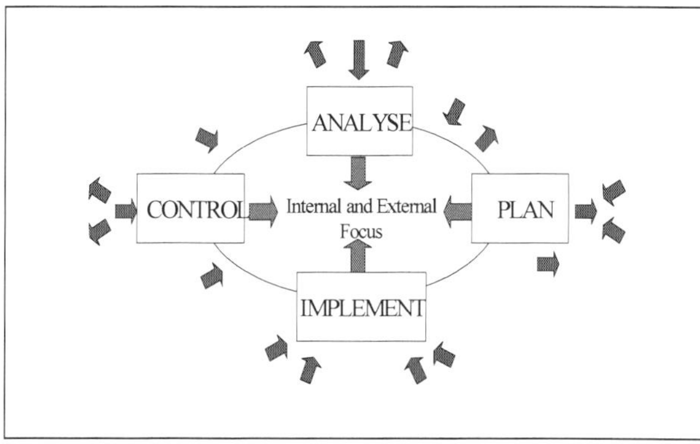

The finance function has no monopoly over the means of achieving corporate performance. Its increasingly widening roles however enhances its potential to facilitate the attainment of high level organizational performance. How enterprises achieve their objectives varies depending on context and business circumstances. Different firms pursue different objectives via different roles accorded to their finance function. This book aims to explain approaches to strategic finance to enable growth of corporate performance. The finance function in high performing organisations continuously alters in line with evolving management expectations and changes in the business environment. What is essential for effective management cannot be pre-defined. Systems in place, operational priorities and circumstances, the values of managers and market challenges all play a role in affecting judgment about what is required to achieve high performance. What corporate performance and organizational excellence signifies is always enterprise-specific, as well as transient over time and subject to managerial judgment. Strategic finance activities are thereby organizationally grounded and dynamic. No book or instructional resource should be taken as providing definitive solutions. The intent of this book is to show the potential of strategic finance thinking. Operationalizing strategic finance will reflect your own assessment of how its fundamentals can be adapted to your enterprise circumstances.

In most companies, there exists shared responsibility for financial work and the operation of control systems. Finance and accounting teams participate more and more with others in the management of the business in many firms across many countries. Consequently, non-financial executives are becoming increasingly aware of financial issues and vice-versa. Greater emphasis is also being placed in many organizations on the use of emerging technologies and systems as 'enablers' of commercial and administrative control activities as well as revenues generation possibilities. Understanding these technologies is thus a growing part of effective managerial control. Coming to grips with operational knowledge is as much a responsibility of finance professionals as is developing an understanding of strategy and control.

There are many factors that affect how financial management relates to and works with the rest of the business. These include the culture and history of the organization, the way in which the business is organised, the influence and personal style of both the chief finance or accounting officer and the chief executive, and the measurement practices adopted. In addition, an important consideration for the finance function revolves around achieving a fine balance between the organizational climate and how it aligns with the ethos of financial control practices. Of essence here is how far the finance function is able to integrate and support other business activities and units whilst attuning itself to a productive cultural balance.

There are businesses which consider that to create and sustain competitive advantage, it is desirable to ensure the effective execution of core business processes – that is, those key processes which generate an outcome valued by customers. In supporting the effective design and operation of the core business processes, strategic finance activities focus on ways to enhance service, quality and cost control in such enterprises. The finance function is uniquely positioned to aid the process by which measures are established to help the business convert strategy into performance. Information can be collected from diverse sources to provide what might be an organizationally balanced view of business performance, which may incorporate a range of measures including customer perspectives, non-financial measures, organizational learning and business environment indicators. In addition, in some enterprises, it may be desirable for the measures to be as consistent as possible throughout the organization and to track performance across core business processes as well as separate auxiliary functions. Performance measurement systems have been of principal importance to finance and accounting specialists traditionally. With on-going changes in the organizational environment, such systems are rapidly being transformed. They are in a state of transition which is guided by changing ideas of acceptable or desirable corporate performance and organizational excellence.

Some companies are moving toward quite specific structures for the finance function. For instance a number of global firms are opting for:
- small numbers of highly skilled finance professionals working as a part of management teams to develop strategy, plan the business and manage performance;
- specialist technicians responsible for ensuring that integrity of financial transactions and management information is maintained throughout distributed and integrated systems, most of which are run by external service providers.
- Data scientists who help unlock insights hidden in data to drive managerial thinking and decisions

Empirical research indicates that many firms are experiencing an increase in the use of financial control and management accounting techniques but changes in the way these are used whereby a more business and support-oriented perspective is replacing the traditional monitoring and control stance. Financial considerations link with both operating concerns and the strategic priorities of enterprises. In many firms, business managers work alongside financial people in cross-functional teams. The trend is indicative of financial professionals needing communication, interpersonal and analytical skills combined with broad strategic and business knowledge. They work within cross-functional teams, have extensive face-to-face communication with people throughout their organization, and are more actively involved in decision-making. They also take on leadership roles in their teams. They may be seen as management advisors or internal consultants.

There is great diversity in the ways in which organizations structure themselves and how their finance function is designed and run. In this sense, as noted above, finance is highly dependent on context. Some organizations opt for a functional form with a dedicated financial management function. Others attempt to achieve the advantages of both centralised and decentralised approaches via small teams of specialists at the centre, strong analytical and advisory support at business unit or process level, and the establishment of service centres for volume transaction processing on behalf of a number of business units. In addition, some functions will be outsourced. There is no ideal strategic finance function structure. The requisite however for adding value is operational and managerial engagement.

Yesterday's Strategy – Tomorrow's Commodity

History does not always teach lessons for extrapolation. Prior to the industrial revolution, artisans and craftsmen used their own land, tools and their hands to produce goods. These were sold in bulk to merchants who paid a market determined piece rate. Once industrialisation began to alter production processes, some factors of production became separated from those who produced. An employer owned the physical premises and the machinery and hired workers. Dissociating land, labour and capital was accompanied by a need to cost labour processes. Cost standards emerged to determine the price of processes so they could be summed to arrive at the cost of products. There were labour costs, material costs and overhead costs reflective of the cost of the premises and operational expenses. The business strategy of the employer differed from that of the merchant. A different organization structure had to be adopted to align with the strategy and novel accounting techniques surfaced. During the nineteenth century many firms did much more than just produce. They purchased ownership of the supply of raw material and they bought into the wholesale function – sometimes extending themselves in retail activities. Spanning a greater depth of control in the value chain was a business strategy that required a different organisational structure. Accounting mechanisms altered. In the early decades of the twentieth century, many firms set up divisions operating across diverse, distinct and sometimes unrelated activities. Their structures changed and new forms of accounting approaches emerged. For long, strategic business changes drove new forms of organizational structures which in turn shaped accounting innovations. In the present new economic environment where technological changes and digitization have altered business strategies, organizational forms and their boundaries it is not clear what accounting techniques follow or indeed whether they themselves direct strategy and structural changes. In the context of strategy-finance links, the past does not show pathways to specific desirable changes.

Over the past six decades, it is clear that technology has impacted how finance professionals collect and report data and the technology itself has altered the results of financial management. Since the end of the Second World War there has been a massive change in the way in which financial transactions are processed. Technological advances have had a huge impact on the number of staff required and on the complexity of financial management techniques and information provision. The technical developments that have taken place and the accounting techniques that have emerged may be summarised as follows:

1950s
- card-posting ledger machines with no calculating capability or card sorting/printing machines;
- calculation by comptometer operator;
- labour was cheap and plentiful, detailed <u>standard costing</u> systems were built, requiring large numbers of staff to drive them.

1960s
- punched card-driven computers and magnetic stripe ledger posting machines;
- electronic calculators;
- standard costing systems reached their peak.

1970s
- mainframe computers became widely used;
- beginnings of financial modelling;
- financial <u>application packages</u> became available;

1980s
- computer performance/price capability escalated dramatically;
- personal computers/spreadsheets became universal with major increases in productivity of management accounting staff;
- standard costing systems became too expensive to maintain and

started to decline;
- activity-based costing generated interest;
- functionality of financial application packages became almost universally accepted.

1990s
- move from mainframe to distributed computer systems;
- trend towards financial transaction processing centres within distributed environment serving many subsidiaries/countries;
- functional transaction processing becoming more and more integrated and embedded in operational (e.g., manufacturing, sales and marketing) systems;
- escalating demand from management for better performance measurement systems and improvements to budgeting and forecasting, met in part by development of activity-based management, strategic cost analysis and the pursuit of more balanced scorecard measures.

2000 and beyond
- the increased use of web-based technologies to link intra- and extra-organizational processes;
- altered economies of scale and scope being effected by organizational reconfigurations;
- enhanced core value focus and interconnectedness via different information routings and accelerated information exchange possibilities;
- systematic knowledge sharing and the management of knowledge assets;
- Less focus on accounting data and more on 'big data';
- Reduced links between costs and revenues with the growth of social media;
- Increased concern with corporate governance as a value driving activity rather than a resource consuming one.

The first decade of the twenty-first century has already resulted in changes on a significant scale. The advent of internet-based commercial approaches are driven in part by technological changes in hardware structures, software platforms and the emergence of altered economics of information retrieval, processing and presentation. Technological advances and the application of innovative business models within the emerging digital economy is giving rise to novel modes of organizational functioning, enterprise management and, new cost management practices. The digital economy is currently transitioning to a more complex and socially engaged web environment. Social media and the growth of digital interface is sponsoring the genesis of altered business models and a fundamental separation of cost drivers from revenue generators.

What is clear also is that standard costing systems were at one stage part of a new strategy. Ultimately their wide scale adoption turned them into commodities. No organization could extract abnormally high profits by virtue of this costing approach. When complexity of production and product diversity became a new corporate strategy enabled by advanced technologies, activity based costing gave some firms an advantage over others in decision making. The widespread adoption of activity accounting made it a commodity. One might make similar inferences about quality costing, the balanced scorecard and target cost management. Thus accounting techniques in and of themselves will not confer strategic advantages – at least not for long. But their contextual deployment with an understanding of complex and unique organizational circumstances proffer the ability to engage in highly competitive finance-based action. This is the role of strategic finance.

In many organizations, convention has taken a back seat. What may in the past have been thought of as a necessary internal activity has been rethought. For instance, many companies have outsourced transaction processing and database maintenance and storage – important activities but not ones which are likely to yield competitive advantages for companies undertaking them in-house. Remote outsourcing is a growing option in the emerging digitised economy where it often makes sense to devolve operational accounting and information processing to an off-base service provider which leverages its core strengths cheaply and effectively. The enterprise is then free to focus on its own core functions and expertise whilst containing costs of secondary activities. But many enterprises also choose to ultimately outsource what they once regarded as core strengths. The role of strategic finance within such enterprise contexts is to continue to point to new orders of organizational excellence and corporate performance.

What Strategic Finance Can Achieve

Today's strategic financial management initiatives are both intense and organizationally complex and as a consequence, necessitate an understanding of and engagement with effective enterprise management. Calls by management commentators for finance function changes to achieve organizational effectiveness is echoed by many companies' senior management teams where this function is valued. Advocates of change for the finance function presume the ability of finance professionals to make a valuable contribution by raising awareness of the strategic possibilities for the organization and by providing a framework for possible implementation.

The finance function is increasingly expected to:
- develop an understanding of the strategic goals of the organization and the ways in which change initiatives contribute to those goals;
- identify current financial management practices that are most complementary to the company's desired change initiatives;
- assess hard, soft and on-line sources of information in order to keep current on strategic change initiatives, best practices and competitive performance metrics;
- develop manager focused strategic control initiatives, including interfaces between strategic, financial and managerial domains;
- identify reliable in-house and external professional sources that can resolve cost containment and core/non-core activity fulfilment;
- establish a due diligence corporate policy, and an approval framework for corporate financial management initiatives;
- communicate on-going changes to senior management as well as to other segments of the business organization.

The role of the strategic finance professional in organizations is to contribute to:
- sensitising top management to risk management exposures and responsibilities;
- setting objectives regarding corporate strategy and policy choices;
- providing financial planning to aid corporate strategy and

asset/liability management;
- identifying underlying business risks and financial exposures;
- formulating and managing hedging strategies for financial and operating risks, using various capital and debt structure alternatives and incorporating tax aspects of derivatives applications;
- collaborating with the treasury function, particularly with regard to transfer pricing and multi-currency accounting ;
- controlling policy implementation;
- providing internal accounting for reporting and control of operations;
- understanding the potential of data intelligence and determining pathways to profit from data access and analysis;
- integrating performance measurement and incentive structures.

Such activities span very wide financial management responsibilities and expertise. Many enterprises seek skills in accounting and finance that are highly technical but that ground an understanding of the practice of management in the operational functions of the business. This translates into enhancing a comprehension of marketing, sales, production, distribution, research and development plus other support functions such as human resources and IT. As an increasing number of companies move to a more process-oriented and digitised operational environment, the finance professional will be required to understand and support emerging forms of web enabled and networked organizational structuring. Similarly, a rapprochement between the marketing and finance function has surfaced firmly in many enterprises.

What seems evident is that time brings with it pressures for changing the finance function which accord with different views of what makes organizations excellent. When business commentators began to speak of a 'new economy', past conceptions of proper organizational management and economic logic were questioned. Liberalisation from what had been deemed essential by many old industrial firms has been sought by new as well as established enterprises to enable faster, leaner and more effective performance. To some, the rise of the internet has made many 'modern' management techniques outdated. Internet technologies and new digital-based business models are driving more changes. Different sections of the book capture the potential of different aspects of strategic finance in a rapidly changing management and business landscape. Various forces have led to strategic finance practices in an economic climate where achieving enhanced enterprise performance is essential. The following chapters discuss established and emerging strategic finance practices deployed by firms in their pursuit of enterprise excellence.

2

PROFIT AND RISK

In 2009, India's Tata Group launched the Nano – the least expensive production car in the world. It was priced at $2000. The Gujarat based plant has the capacity to produce 250000 Nanos a year. Tata ships about 70000 a year – an underwhelming response. What went wrong? In part, rising interest rates, higher fuel prices, internal production problems and increased material costs. Today the car sells at closer to $3000. This has priced out the intended first-time car buyers with no regular employment or payslips to support credit applications. Many of those who can afford to buy the Nano have opted for slightly more sophisticated vehicles because of Tata's emphasis on the Nano's cheapness and its very basic features. The anticipated revenues have not been forthcoming, 'frugal engineering' proved unable to combat unintended cost increases, the market has presented unintended risks. How profitable the Nano will prove to be for Tata remains to be seen.

Costing Things

Assessing risk is a conditioned reflex for most people. Deciding on one course of action as opposed to another usually involves evaluating the value placed on the desired outcome and weighing this against the burden of taking the action and an evaluation of possible unintended effects. Financial decisions assume generally that the rewards anticipated should take account of the risks absorbed. A sure thing carries little risk so the payoff should be smaller than the returns expected to arise from a risky proposition because of the chance that the returns could be lower. A remote payoff means a greater wait for the returns and higher risks that they may not accrue and so the size of the hope for payoff should be sufficiently large to encourage the investment to take place. Ultimately risk-return relationships should seem equitable. An enterprise which finds ways of more certain high returns for the same degree of risk will achieve abnormally high profit performance. One that underestimated the risk of higher than expected costs or softer revenues attainment will see its profits lag.

Profit is a measure of a payoff. Before thinking about risk, some idea of how profit is measured is essential. In most enterprises, profit is regarded in economic terms as the difference between revenues and costs. Consequently, measurements of revenues and costs are essential. We focus here initially on cost issues and then turn our attention to revenues.

Many innovative financial management techniques have been used by global enterprises over the past two decades. Examples are backflush accounting, activity-based costing, target cost management, quality costing and life cycle costing. Subsequent chapters discuss these and others. Established management concepts relating to profit and costing issues find usage in many organizations today. These are considered in this section. The starting point is to understand cost behaviour concepts.

There is little doubt that costs concern everyone and that an awareness of costs can change human behaviour. Costs themselves exhibit different types of behaviour depending on the enterprise activities being carried out. Activities can include production, sales generated, distance travelled, orders processed and so on. The relationship between costs and activities is of concern to all managers. Some organizations use an extremely quantitative approach to managing people, activities and resources. Davenport (2010) reports that some enterprises "compete on analytics" not because they can but because they should. Analytics refers to sophisticated quantitative and statistical analysis and predictive modelling supported by data-savvy experts using powerful information technology. These organizations know what products people want, what prices they want to pay for them, how many they will purchase in their lifetime and what will make them buy more. They also know compensation costs and employee turnover rates and costs in addition to how much personnel contribute to or detract from the bottom line and how salary levels relate to individual performance. Although these organizations make heavy use of calculative information, for analytically minded leaders, the challenge is when to know that they have to run with the numbers and when to simply appeal to intuition. Examples of such companies are Yahoo!, Amazon.com, Wal-Mart, Dell, Capital One, Honda, Intel, Marriott and Barclays among many others. Analytics allows these and other firms to aggressively leverage their data in major business decisions and processes to achieve high corporate performance. There is some evidence that in many enterprises large data examination and business analytics undertaken as a guide to decision making results in productivity gains and yields higher returns on equity (Brynjolfsson and McAfee, 2011).

How far do companies compete by controlling costs? IBM is confronting globalisation-based competition by reorganizing its workforce and rethinking its supply structure. In less than three years, it increased its employees in India five-fold to benefit from lower cost data centres, software development, call centres and research. Its workforce in China, Brussels and Eastern Europe doubled over this period. IBM also calculates that automation investments can cut more than 10% from its outsourcing costs. Consider also Lego which turned itself around from losses exceeding $300 million to profitability with a year partly by eliminating product elements which people had developed personal attachments to. In the motor car industry, Ford benchmarks its costs with those of its more profitable competitors: it measures its per-vehicle cost disadvantage with Toyota. Likewise, Porsche which own over 30% of Volkswagen is sharing its expertise in cost control: Porsche's profit margin exceeds 19% whilst that of Volkswagen is well under 3%. Carlos Ghosn who heads Renault and Nissan and who is the highest paid CEO in Europe has an extreme quantitative results-oriented approach whereby numerical targets are set for which his staff are then held accountable for achieving. He is commonly know as "le cost killer!"

Costs and Expenses

Finance executives understand well that to ask, "what does it cost?" can be a rhetorical question. For this reason, they often use the expression: "Different costs for different purposes" to recognise that judgment must be exercised in choosing how a cost is determined depending on what managerial need is to be served. As a starting point, it is useful to consider what a cost is by definition. A cost may be defined as the monetary measure given up to acquire a product. Managers refer to a wide array of cost categories. Many of these appear in this book. In discussing financial statements, one often identifies the timing of cost incursion in terms of the past, the present and the future by referring to historical, current and budgeted costs. Some costs may be expired and appear as expenses in a profit and loss statement (e.g.: electricity, lighting and heating expenses). Other costs may result from expenditures whereby assets are acquired with a view to generating income and remain unexpired as they await expensing (e.g.: the cost of a building or machine). Such unexpired costs are typically referred to as <u>assets</u> in the balance sheet of a company. The immediate purpose here is to describe how costs behave as changes in activities take place. Sometimes this entails describing how an expense arises as an unexpired cost becomes expired, such as for example, when a machine loses part of its value and future usefulness in producing items that are sold to customers.

Accountants typically recognise two main types of cost behaviour patterns: Fixed and Variable. A cost that varies directly in a one-to-one manner with changes in activity is referred to as a <u>variable cost</u>. The variable cost per unit does not ordinarily change as activity levels change. Examples of variable costs include material costs as production takes place, electricity costs to power a machine and sales commissions based on revenues as sales progress. If a product A requires £5 of direct materials per unit then the total direct materials cost of manufacturing 10,000 units is £50,000; 20,000 units require direct materials of £100,000, and so on. The unit cost of the direct materials (£5) remains constant with changes in volume, but total variable costs increase with increased activity. By contrast, a <u>fixed cost</u> is one which remains constant in total terms but which diminishes at the unit level as activity levels increase. Examples of fixed costs include a machine's monthly depreciation charge, a supervisor's annual salary or a quarterly insurance bill. The straight-line depreciation (i.e. the assumed diminution every year) of £200,000 on factory buildings and equipment will not change, regardless of whether 10,000 units or 20,000 units of product are manufactured. Outside the <u>relevant range</u> of activities, further fixed costs may have to be incurred. Although fixed costs do not vary in total with changes in volume of activity, the unit cost will change with changes in activity. If volume increases, the unit cost will decrease, and if volume decreases, the unit cost will increase. Thus, the unit cost of straight-line depreciation of £200,000 for 10,000 units is £20, and for 20,000 units of product, the unit cost is £10.

It is well to note that both variable and fixed costs exhibit the particular cost behaviour they describe only over defined relevant ranges. Thus, the variable cost per unit stays the same only over a relevant range of activities over which changes in the marginal cost per unit arising from economies of scale, increased productivity or operating inefficiencies are considered negligible. The supply price of packaging material may fall once a certain volume purchase triggers a set discount. Likewise, fixed costs will likely remain fixed only until the capacity of the resource giving rise to the cost is attained. Thus if a supermarket manager can only supervise ten customers, a second supervisor will have to be hired if between eleven and twenty cashiers are to be supervised. In this instance, the relevant range of the supervisor is for ten cashiers. Such a situation can give rise to stepwise cost increases (sometimes referred to as semi-fixed costs). Of course, if the relevant range for a fixed cost category diminishes, at some point, the cost behaviour may be more appropriately considered a variable cost – again with its own relevant range.

There are costs which cannot be treated as purely fixed or variable, but which combine an element of both forms of cost behaviour. Mixed (or semi-variable) costs do not stay constant as activity levels change, nor do they vary proportionately with such changes. Rather, they may increase, but only in part, with increased activity. Consider, for example, a mobile phone for which a periodic standing charge is payable in addition to a talk-time related charge. The total cost of the mobile phone per period would reflect both a fixed and variable cost component. The same would be true of a commissioned salesperson earning a base salary whereby the base salary would be a fixed cost to the employer and the variable cost component would stem from, say, a commission on total sales over a period. What is clear is that cost behaviour classification relies in large part, on approximations as to costs, relevant ranges and activity levels. Ascribing behaviour to costs is not always a precise endeavour but it can lead to useful cost and financial management applications.

The Components of Product Costs

All products can be broken down into different cost components. Sometimes managers are interested in attaching costs to departments or processes or hierarchical levels via their organizations. Whatever the foci of cost attachment, such points are referred to as cost objects. If it is possible to clearly trace costs to a cost object then such costs are viewed as being direct. Conversely, if costs can only be allocated by more or less arbitrary methods of assignment then such costs are viewed as being indirect to the cost object.

Very often, costs associated with different cost objects in service organizations are indirect. A service cannot be inventoried or stored and therefore the product cost must be seen as representing the accumulation of many <u>indirect costs</u>. Manufacturing organizations engage in the active production of products to be sold such that many costs accumulate at the level of chosen cost objects in a more immediate and demonstrable manner. Thus cost objects in manufacturing organizations often comprise many <u>direct costs</u>.

For a manufactured product, much of the raw material can be expected to be demonstrably traceable to the product. If it is convenient and economic to do so, then such material input represents <u>direct material costs</u>. There may of course be costs which could be traced to the product but only with difficulty of measurement and which would not yield information that could be viewed as economically viable to collect or material to management decisions (a £2,000 exercise to trace £100 more accurately is not justifiable). Such theoretically traceable direct costs are in practice often treated as if they were indirect costs and regarded as part of overhead costs.

<u>Direct labour costs</u> consist of wages paid to employees in production or service environments. These costs are referred to as direct because they are directly traceable to the service or the product in an economically feasible way. They may be assumed to be variable with activity levels if, over relatively small time frames, direct labour costs can be increased or reduced. There are many situations of course where such a perspective on direct labour costs would be difficult to uphold. For instance, if direct labour is really seen to be near-permanent because of difficulties in recruiting once workers are let go then it may be preferable to regard the labour resource as a fixed cost.

Although it may be possible to directly trace a labour cost category to a product or service, the question of whether it is desirable to do so must be considered. The production of an item may require post-production labour costs to be incurred for clean-up. In theory, it may be possible to ascribe the cleaning costs to the product but the company may simply prefer to treat this cost genre as <u>indirect labour</u>. Moreover, many companies making use of automated technologies now have a very small proportion of direct labour costs which they prefer to treat as fixed. Across many industries, the proportion of direct labour costs as part of the total costs of products or services is declining. This is probably due to the generally inverse relationship that exists between capital intensiveness and labour intensiveness. Investments into flexible organizational technologies (see next section) such as computer assisted design and computer aided manufacturing systems as well as flexible manufacturing systems and industrial robots mean that production processes and many operational activities can take place using lower and lower levels of labour input.

Factory overhead costs refer to those which cannot directly be traced to the provision of a service or the manufacture of a product because this would be too difficult or too expensive to do (or both). Effectively, factory overhead costs include all production costs except direct material and labour costs. Part of the overhead costs for a department or for a process may vary with activity levels and therefore be viewed as variable, whereas others may be fixed over defined activity levels. Such costs which combine fixed and variable resource elements may be regarded as mixed and require extricating one type of cost from the other to make managerially useful decisions.

Reflections on Cost Behaviour

The passage of time is a most important consideration in the application of financial management concepts. In a broad sense, time has altered the uses cost information is put to. Whereas traditionally, knowledge of costs primarily served a recording and stewardship function until relatively recently, today costing information is in many contexts considered as business intelligence. But intelligent behaviour does not necessarily follow from a knowledge of cost behaviour! It is our conception of time periodization which demarcates the relevance of costs. Accurate but untimely costing information may be of less use than on-time cost approximations. In the context of applying our knowledge of cost behaviour in enterprise management, it must be recognised that in the long run, costs are largely decision-driven and certainly are all variable. The usefulness of cost behaviour concepts is therefore largely dependent on prior knowledge of the managerial motivation for desiring to know a cost. The behaviour of costs may be estimated using a variety of approaches. Some commonly used methods are considered below.

A basic method of cost estimation is <u>account classification</u>. This procedure requires a limited amount of data and relies heavily on professional judgement. When this method is used, the finance executive obtains actual production and cost data for a single period. Each production cost account is analysed to determine its status as fixed, variable or semi-variable (i.e., a cost which has both a fixed and a variable component). All costs are classified as fixed or variable and are totalled across these two categories. In order to do this, a subjective estimate must be made of the variable and fixed portion of semi-variable costs (or mixed). Variable unit production costs are estimated by dividing total variable costs by the number of units produced. The following cost estimating equation is derived:

$$\hat{y} = ax + b$$

where $\hat{y}$ is the estimated total cost, a the estimated variable unit cost, b the estimated fixed costs (if the range of observed activity points covers zero), and x the number of units produced (or the activity in question which is thought to relate to cost incursions). The 'cap' is inserted over the dependent variable y to indicate that the equation is used to estimate total costs. An actual value of y may not equal the estimated $\hat{y}$.

An alternative is the <u>engineering</u> approach which requires various physical inputs to be assessed. For example, material input can be estimated by analysing product blueprints and specifications. Likewise, a specific operation may be deemed to be achievable using say 0.8 direct labour hours. This would represent a standard based on natural working conditions, using perhaps a specific machine and assuming the deployment of a trained worker who can comfortably maintain the required pace of work as part of her ordinary functions. The engineering method can clearly be expensive to use but it does not rely on the availability of past data on operations or productivity.

If it is assumed that there is only one relevant independent variable (x above), then a <u>scattergraph</u> analysis might be used to separate a mixed cost into its fixed and variable components. To perform such an analysis, the actual observations made are graphed and cost behaviour is visually estimated. Suppose, for instance, that the following data are available for total costs versus units produced:

Costs	Units
£500	48
£600	62
£650	66
£700	68
£770	79

Figure 2.1 provides **a rough representation of the situation because it would be drawn manually and would rely on the interpretation and judgement of the individual doing the estimations. A slight variation of the method is the <u>high-low</u> approach, which makes use of just two observations (the highest and the lowest activities points) in constructing the estimating line. Clearly, no judgement is required here but the method is likely to yield improbable results if the two points happen to be outliers.**

Intelligent Regression

<u>Simple linear regression</u> (also termed 'least squares analysis'), takes the estimating line as represented by the above form of the equation. It assumes that there is a single independent variable (x) and that the relationship between it and the dependent variable (y) is linear. The objective is to construct a good fitting line through all the data points that are available. Regression is based on mathematical principles that ensure a best-fitting line. To further understand the method, it is necessary to consider how 'best' is operationally defined. Many statistical computer packages and hand-held calculators will process the sample data to provide values for a and b in the equation above.

Figure 2.1 A Scattergraph

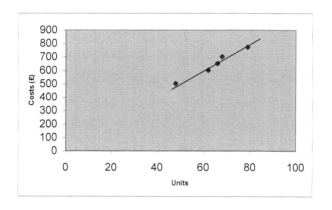

Suppose the following data were available:

Production volume (units)	Labour costs (£)
105	990
44	460
61	600
42	440
77	740
78	760
87	850
31	330
103	1,000
84	810
53	540
40	430
56	560
37	390
69	670
93	930

For the particular set of data for x and y values, the regression equation would be:

$$\hat{y} = 60.48 + 0.8955x$$

Although regression identifies the best-fitting line using a given variable and a given data set, it does not ensure that the equation is useful. There is a burden on the user to select appropriate variables for the analysis. The mere fact that a least squares best-fitting line can be derived from two sets of data should not be taken to suggest causality or even some logical association between the two.

The <u>coefficient of determination</u> (r^2) is one indicator of the potential usefulness of a regression equation. This value will range between 0 and 1 and is a measure of the goodness of the fit of the line to the sample data (for the above example, $r^2 = 0.89$). The higher the r^2 the better, but correlation does not imply causality. Two variables can be highly correlated but need not be causally related. Thus, professional judgement needs to be exercised in selecting independent variables.

The r^2 statistic can be useful in deciding which of several possible regression equations should be selected. For example, suppose overhead costs have been regressed with (1) direct labour hours and (2) machine hours. The equation with the highest r^2 value would be a favoured candidate assuming that the r^2 is significant, i.e., exceeds 0.3 (and that other statistics for the regression model are not in conflict with this conclusion).

Where there is a choice between using different independent variables that are deemed equally useful, the organization may opt for one over the others on the basis of ease of collection. Another relevant statistic to consider is the standard error of the estimate (s_e) which is a measure of the 'average' difference between the actual observations of the dependent variable in the sample and the values predicted by the regression equation. It essentially signals the extent of 'scatter' – around the calculated regression line. A lower value is thus preferable to a high value (the value for the above example is 8.47, which is relatively small). Another useful statistic is the standard error of the estimated coefficient a (s_a). This statistic is a measure of the sampling error that results from estimating the true coefficient that exists in the population. It is reflective of the uncertainty of the slope of the calculated regression line. Again, the lower the value, the better.

Regression analysis can be a useful tool for estimating costs and can be used as a forecasting technique for certain management decisions. It is important to recognise that it relies on assumptions. One limitation is the range of values for which the equation should be used. The results can be misleading when used to estimate costs for values of the independent variable that are outside the range observed in the sample. Attempting to extrapolate outside this range has its problems in that the real relationship may be very different from that within the range. This is why the intercept term (b) cannot be taken to infer a plausible fixed cost level if the original observation points did not include a reading at zero activity level. It is important also to note that simple regression assumes there is a linear relationship between the two variables in the population. The model will fit a straight line to the data even if the actual relationship is not linear.

Achieving profitability

Once costs have been classified into their fixed and variable categories by financial executives, their effects on profit, by considering revenues and volume, can be explored. Cost-volume-profit (CVP) analysis is a technique which can be used to indicate the revenues necessary to just match the total costs in carrying out operations or to indicate the revenues or sales unit level necessary to achieve a desired or target profit.

The point in the operations of an enterprise at which revenues and expired costs are exactly equal is called the break-even point. At this level of operations, an enterprise will neither realise an operating income nor incur an operating loss. Break-even analysis can be applied to past periods but is most useful when visualising future performance scenarios as a guide to business planning. When concerned with future prospects and future operations, the approach relies upon estimates. The reliability of the analysis is thus greatly influenced by the accuracy of the estimates.

The break-even point can be computed by means of a mathematical formula which indicates the relationship between revenue, costs and capacity. The data required are:

(i) total estimated fixed costs for a future period, such as a year;

(ii) the total estimated variable costs for the same period, stated as a percentage of net sales.

The starting point is the profit equation:

Profit = Sales − Costs

= (Selling Price per Unit x Quantity) − (Variable costs + Fixed Costs)

Naturally, if Sales = Costs, the entity does not generate profits. Knowing the point of activity where this occurs is useful to managers.

Examples of CVP in action

Assume that an organization's fixed costs are estimated at £90,000 and that the expected variable costs are 60 per cent of sales. The maximum sales at 100 per cent capacity are £400,000. The break-even point is £225,000 of sales, computed as follows:

Break-even sales (£) = Fixed costs (£) + Variable costs
(as % break-even sales)
S = £90,000 + 60%S
40%S = £90,000
S = £225,000

The Profit and Loss statement would look like this:
Sales		£225,000
Expenses:		
Variable costs (£225,000 x 60%)	£135,000	
Fixed costs	£90,000	£225,000
Operating profit		0

This is also shown in the graph in Figure 2.2. The break-even point can be expressed either in terms of total sales or in terms of units of sales. For example, if the unit selling price is £25, the break-even point can be expressed as either £225,000 of sales or 9,000 units (£225,000/£25). The break-even point can be affected by changes in the fixed costs, unit variable costs and unit selling price.

Figure 2.2 Cost-Volume-Profit graph

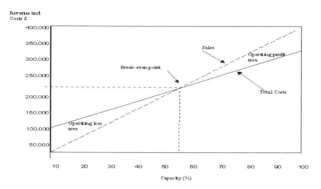

At the break-even point, sales and costs are exactly equal. By modifying the break-even equation, the sales volume required to earn a desired amount of profit may be estimated. For this purpose, a factor for desired profit is added to the standard break-even formula.

Consider a situation in which fixed costs are estimated at £200,000, variable costs are estimated at 60 per cent of sales, and the desired profit is £100,000. The sales volume is £750,000, computed as follows:

Sales (£) = Fixed costs (£) + Variable costs (as % sales) + Desired profit

S = £200,000 + 60%S + £100,000
40% S = £300,000
S = £750,000

The validity of the computation is shown as follows:

Sales		£750,000
Expenses:		
Variable costs (£750,000 x 60%)	£450,000	
Fixed costs	£200,000	£650,000
Operating profit		£100,000

The break-even point for an enterprise selling two or more products can be calculated on the basis of a specified sales mix. If the sales mix is assumed to be constant, the break-even point and the sales necessary to achieve desired levels of operating profit can be readily calculated.

Consider the following data for the CVP Company:

Product	Selling price per unit	Variable cost per unit	Sales mix
A	£90	£70	80%
B	£140	£95	20%
Fixed costs = £200,000			

To compute the break-even point when several products are sold, it is useful to think of the individual products as contributing to a weighted average product W. These computations are as follows:
Unit selling price of W: (£90 x 0. 8) + (£140 x 0. 2) = £100
Unit variable cost of W: (£70 x 0. 8) + (£95 x 0. 2) = £75

The variable costs for product W are therefore expected to be 75 per cent of sales (£75/£100). The break-even point can be determined in the normal manner using the equation as follows:
Break-even sales (£) = Fixed costs (£) + Variable costs (as % of break-even sales)
Break-even sales S = £200,000 + 75% S
Break-even sales 25% S = £200,000
Break-even sales S = £800,000

The break-even point of £800,000 of sales of enterprise product W is equivalent to 8,000 total sales units (£800,000/£100). Since the sales mix for products A and B is 80 per cent and 20 per cent respectively, the break-even quantity of A is 6400 units (8000 x 80%) and for B it is 1,600 units (8,000 x 20%) units. A verification of the analysis is given in Table 2.1.

Table 2.1 CVP Company Income Statement for Year

	Product A	Product B	Total	
Sales				
6,400 units x £90	£576,000		£576,000	
1,600 units x £140		£224,000	£224,000	
Total sales	£576,000	£224,000		£800,000
Variable costs				
6,400 units x £70	£448,000		£448,000	
1,600 units x £95		£152,000	£152,000	
Total variable costs	£448,000	£152,000		£600,000
Fixed costs			£200,000	
Total costs				£800,000
Operating profit				£ 0

The reliability of cost-volume-profit analysis depends upon the validity of several assumptions. One major assumption is that there is no change in stock quantities during the year – that is, the quantity of units in the beginning stock equals the quantity of units in the ending stock. When changes in stock quantities occur, the computations for cost-volume-profit analysis become more complex.

For cost-volume-profit analysis, a relevant range of activity is assumed within which all costs can be classified as either fixed or variable. Within the relevant range, which is usually a range of activity over which the company is likely to operate, the unit variable costs and the total fixed costs will not change. Moreover, the sales mix remains constant for a multi-product environment.

Contribution Margin Analysis

The classification of costs according to the way in which they behave enables particular types of short run decision to be made (i.e., one year or less). Contribution margin analysis relies on an appreciation of fixed versus variable cost components. Contribution margin represents sales net of variable costs. In other words, the contribution margin represents the amount available to cover fixed costs for a period and ultimately to produce a profit. The application of a contribution margin computation for a special order decision is provided by The Godzilla Company.

The Godzilla Company which manufactures a specialty electronic toy has developed the following predetermined unit cost estimates at a production and sales volume of 25,000 units:

Direct materials	£20
Direct labour	£15
Variable factory overhead	£5
Fixed factory overhead	£10
Variable selling and administrative	£5
Fixed selling and administrative	£2
Total	£57

A special order has been received from a foreign distributor to purchase 2000 units at £47 each. The company has sufficient excess capacity and does not currently compete in any foreign market. Accepting the special order will result in special selling and administrative expenses of £500. There will be no additional variable-selling and administrative expenses. Should the order be accepted?

The relevant unit costs are direct materials, direct labour and variable factory overhead. They total £40 per unit. Hence, the unit contribution margin if the order is accepted is £7. The total contribution margin of £14,000 (£7 x 2000) far exceeds the contract's fixed costs of £500. Accordingly, the contract contributes £13,500 to common fixed costs and profits. The relevant costs to include in the analysis are the incremental costs of the contract, and not the allocated fixed costs.

Suppose now that Godzilla can reduce the direct materials cost by £2 per unit and direct labour costs by £3 per unit if it purchases component GZ99 from a domestic supplier at a cost of £5.50 per unit. Accepting the order will permit Godzilla to rent one of its buildings to a local firm for £20,000 per year. Should Godzilla make or buy component GZ99? The incremental unit cost of buying is £0.50 per unit. However, buying will result in incremental revenues of £20,000 per year. At a volume of 25,000 units, the incremental profit from buying is £20,000 - £0.50(25,000) = £7,500. It appears desirable to buy. Given the focus on incremental costs, this approach to short run decision-making is sometimes referred to as incremental cost analysis. What is important to ask regarding <u>incremental costs</u> is whether the costs differ between the alternative courses of action being considered and whether they relate to the future. Only such costs are deemed 'relevant' in incremental cost analysis.

Standards for Managing Risks

<u>Standard costs</u> provide a useful means for costing products. For a manufacturing company, labour and material costs can often be predetermined to coincide with actual cost incursion. Overhead costs, however, may pose costing problems in that not all overhead costs per unit will be known at any one stage of the financial period. For costing a contract, it is thus useful to determine a volume-based method of allocating overhead costs. The link between overhead cost incursion and a volume variable such as units produced, or labour cost or machine hours worked, can be statistically tested using regression analysis.

Consider the Contract Co., which uses a budgeted overhead rate in applying overhead to production orders on a labour cost basis for Department A and on a machine-hour basis for Department B. At the beginning of Year 1, the company made the following estimations:

	Department A	Department B
Direct labour	£128,000	
Machine-hours		20,000
Factory overhead	£144,000	£150,000
Overhead rates	112.5% of direct labour	£7.50 per machine-hour

During January, the cost record for job order number 500 which consisted of 20 units of product shows the following:

	Department A	Department B
Materials requisitioned	£20	£40
Direct labour cost	£32	£21
Machine-hours		13

The total departmental costs are then determined to obtain the unit product costs:

Department A		Department B	
Raw materials	£20.00	Raw materials	£ 40.00
Direct labour	£32.00	Direct labour	£ 21.00
Factory department overhead applied		Factory department overhead applied	
(32 x 112.5%)	£36.00	(13 x £7.50)	£ 97.50
Total	£88.00		£158.50

Total costs: £88.00 + £158.50 = £246.50
            £246.50 × 20 = £12.325 per unit

An adjustment will likely be made for deviations between budgeted overhead rates and the actual costs incurred. Thus, suppose that at the end of Year 1 it is found that actual factory overhead cost amounts to £160,000 in Department A and £138,000 in Department B and that the actual direct labour cost is £148,000 in Department A and the actual machine-hours are 18,000 in Department B. The over-applied or under-applied overhead amount for each department and for the factory as a whole can be readily calculated:

Department A: Applied overhead
   (112.5% of £148,000)   £ 166,500
   Actual overhead   £ 160,000
   Over-applied overhead   £ 6,500

Department B: Applied overhead
   (18,000 × £7.50)   £ 135,000
   Actual overhead   £ 138,000
   Under-applied overhead   (3,000)
Total over-applied factory overhead   £ 3,500

It is to be noted that the extent of the variances and therefore cost misallocations is dependent principally on the choice of overhead allocation base and the accuracy of the rate at which it is allocated. If the difference is significant in relation to the year end accounts, an adjustment to the overhead value of stock at the year-end can be calculated.

Standard Costing and Variance Analysis

The risk that expectations do not materialize always exists. But managers take such risks. To minimize the adverse impact of deviations from plans, managers often identify the magnitude of these deviations as activities are ongoing. A standard costing system helps manage risks. If deviations or variances from expectations are outside a range thought to be acceptable, managers can take appropriate action.

What is a standard? A standard cost may be defined as the budgeted cost for one unit of a particular resource. One objective of using standard costs is to provide a tool for investigating deviations between expectations and outcomes. The actual profit for a year may differ from plan depending on how far sales and costs have deviated from expected values. The variance between volume expectations and actual activity is also an essential component of the investigation. This requires a consideration of 'flexible' rather than 'static' activity volumes. A useful illustration of the use of standard costs to investigate differences between expectations and outcomes follows.

Suppose that for October, the Redd Co. budgeted sales at 30,000 units at a selling price of £10 each and a variable cost of £6 each. Actual sales were 28,000 units. Table 2.2 shows that net income was £17,000 less than budgeted.

One could conclude that the reduced sales caused net income to be reduced by £20,000. It would appear that variable costs were £5,000 less than expected, helping to offset the reduced sales. However, this is misleading. The £5,000 favourable variance was derived by comparison of the actual costs for 28,000 units with the budgeted costs for 30,000 units. Such a comparison is inappropriate. Costs are expected to be lower if sales are lower. In fact, the firm can reduce variable costs to zero by selling nothing.

It is useful to prepare a flexible budget that shows total variable costs for 28,000 units rather than 30,000 units, at a variable cost per unit of £6. This is illustrated in Table 2.3 which shows that variable costs are not £5,000 favourable but £7,000 unfavourable. In other words, since the company sold only 28,000 units, variable costs should have been only £168,000 (£6 x 28,000 units). Instead, they were £175,000.

Fixed cost variances total £2,000 unfavourable. Notice that the budget for fixed costs is £50,000 in both the 'static' budget (for 30,000 units) and the 'flexible' budget (for 28,000 units). By definition, fixed costs do not change within a relevant range. Assuming a relevant range of 0–50,000 units for Redd Co.'s fixed costs, these costs would be the same for both 28,000 units and 30,000 units of sales. Thus, within the relevant range the flexible budget shows the same amount of fixed costs. However, outside the relevant range, the flexible budget would also show different levels of fixed costs. A detailed analysis of specific items of fixed cost would reveal those costs that resulted in the £2,000 unfavourable variance.

Table 2.2 Redd Co. Income Statement for the Month ended 31 October

	Budget (30,000 units)	Actual (28,000 units)	Variance
Sales	£300,000	£280,000	£20,000 U
Variable costs	£180,000	£175,000	£ 5,000 F
Contribution margin	£120,000	£105,000	£15,000 U
Fixed costs	£ 50,000	£ 52,000	£ 2,000 U
Net income	£ 70,000	£ 53,000	£17,000 U

F = favourable
U = unfavourable.

Table 2.3 Redd Co. Income Statement for the Month ended 31 October

	Budget (28,000 units)	Actual (28,000 units)	Variance
Sales	£280,000	£280,000	—
Variable costs	£168,000	£175,000	£7,000 U
Contribution margin	£112,000	£105,000	£7,000 U
Fixed costs	£ 50,000	£ 52,000	£2,000 U
Net income	£ 62,000	£ 53,000	£9,000 U

Actual net income was £17,000 less than budgeted net income; £9,000 of that £17,000 was caused by variances in costs. Specifically, variable costs were £7,000 more than they should have been for the achieved level of activity, 28,000 units, and fixed costs were £2,000 more than they should have been. The fact that actual sales in units were less than budgeted also caused net income to be less than expected. This difference is referred to as the <u>sales variance</u>. The sales variance shows how much contribution margin was lost because budgeted sales were not achieved. Thus:

Sales variance = (Actual unit sales - Budgeted unit sales) x
                      Contribution margin per unit
Sales variance = (28,000 units - 30,000 units) x £4 per unit
             = - 2,000 units x £4 per unit
             = £8,000 U

The calculation above shows that because sales were 2,000 units less than expected, net income was £8,000 less than expected, resulting in an unfavourable sales variance. The £17,000 unfavourable variance in net income is as follows:

Sales variance	£8,000 U
Variable cost variances	£7,000 U
Fixed cost variances	£2,000 U
Net income variance	£17,000 U

In summary, the company failed to achieve its budgeted net income of £70,000 because lost sales resulted in an £8,000 decrease in expected net income, variable cost variances resulted in a £7,000 decrease in expected net income, and fixed cost variances resulted in a £2,000 decrease in expected net income. The details of these variances can be further analysed to determine more specific reasons why they occurred.

We can view a <u>standard cost system</u> as an accounting system under which all manufacturing costs are charged to production at standard costs. This practice is in contrast to an actual cost system, which charges actual costs to production as they are incurred, or to an actual/normal cost system, which charges actual direct material and direct labour costs to production but charges variable and fixed factory overhead at a predetermined, or standard rate. Consider the following standards for Redd:

Unit Cost
Direct material (2.5 lbs per unit at £0.70 per lb)   £1.75
Direct labour (0.25 hrs per unit at £8 per hr)   £2.00
Factory overhead (0.25 hrs per unit at £4 per DLH)   £1.00
Total standard variable cost per unit   £4.75

For November Redd Co. budgeted production for 12,000 units. However, only 10,000 units were produced. A performance report based on a flexible budget of 10,000 units may be prepared as shown in Table 2.4. The budgeted amounts in the performance report are based on the standard variable costs per unit multiplied by 10,000 units. The performance report shows that the total variable cost variance for November was unfavourable by £2,335.

Table 2.4 Redd Co. Performance Report for the Month ended 30 November

	Budget	Actual	Variance
Direct material	£17,500	£16,900	£ 600 F
Direct labour	£20,000	£21,735	£1,735 U
Variable factory overhead	£10,000	£11,200	£1,200 U
Totals	£47,500	£49,835	£2,335 U

To illustrate how standard costs are used in analysing variances, suppose that Redd Co. is applying variable factory overhead on the basis of direct labour hours rather than the units produced. Table 2.5 indicates the calculations that must be performed in order to obtain variance values for each variable cost category. The actual material and labour costs and quantities used are obtained from the company's records.

Table 2.5 Redd Co. Calculations to Obtain Variance Values

Material price variance

(Actual quantity x Actual price) - (Actual quantity x Standard price)
(AQ x AP) - (AQ x SP)
(26,000 lb x £0.25) - (26,000 x £0.70) = £11,700 F

Material usage variance
(Actual quantity x Standard price) - (Standard quantity allowed for flexible budget x Standard price)
(AQ x SP) - (SQA x SP)
(26,000 x £0.70) - (25,000 lb x £0.70) = £700 U

Labour rate variance
(Actual hours x Actual rate) - (Actual hours x Standard rate)
(AH x AR) - (AH x SR)
(2,700 hr x £8.05) - (2,700 hr x £8.00) = £135 U

Labour efficiency variance
(Actual hours x Standard rate) - (Standard hours allowed for flexible budget x Standard rate)
(AH x SR) x (SAH x SR)
(2,700 hr x £8.00) - (2,500 hr x £8.00) = £1,600 U

Overhead spending variance
Actual cost incurred - (Actual hours x Standard rate)
£11,200 - (2,700 hr x £4.00) = £400 U

Overhead efficiency variance
(Actual hours x Standard rate) - (Standard hours allowed for flexible budget x Standard rate)

(AH x SR) − (SHA x SR)
(2,700 hr x £4.00) − (2,500 hr x £4.00) = £800 U

Individual variances will provide information on the efficiency and effectiveness with which organizational resources are used. The use of standard costing is appropriate for organizations with activities that consist of a series of repetitive operations. This would include many manufacturing organizations. Standard costing cannot be readily applied to activities of a non-repetitive nature as there is little basis within such contexts for observing recurring actions and processes.

Whilst it is possible to extend standard cost-based variance analysis to achieve greater degrees of refinement, an increased focus on the technical complexities of deviations from expectations can lead managers to relegate understandings of expectations to the assessment of deviations. Advocates of change in financial management prefer more strategic analysis rather than technical refinement. An understanding of external forces and their impact on the management of organizational activities is viewed as desirable for enterprise executives across different managerial functions. Enterprises should not crowd out external considerations by paying excessive attention to internal factors as excessive analysis of this type may lead to organizational paralysis.

This section has identified traditional financial management approaches which assist in the analysis of economic inputs and outputs and the determination of profits. These approaches to analysis have the aim of allowing managerial judgment on risks that organizations undertake to yield profits and on ways in which risk management can be best effected. Ultimately, profit-making and risk-taking exist in tandem. Managing the two requires an understanding of how they are constituted.

3

FROM FLEXIBLE TO FLUID ORGANIZATIONS

In April 2013 Google began shipping its "Explorer Edition" of Google Glass for $1,500. Google Glass is eyewear that incorporates a miniature computer with a display attached to its frame - it can shoot pictures, take videos, run apps and deliver information. The interface is controlled by voice recognition, head nods and swipes of a control bar on the side of the glasses. Some tech-industry observers believe that we are years away before Google Glass reaches a price point and convenience level that leads to widespread adoption. The same was said of mobile phones in the 1980s! Google's CEO Larry Page says: "Our goal is to get happy users using Glass...an adventure that may take years." (22/5/2013 in Knowledge@Wharton). There are experts who believe, Google will ultimately monetize Google Glass somehow, most likely through targeted advertising. Others say, if Google Glass succeeds, it could help Google become a hardware player with cutting-edge designs. The power of technology is closely linked to resource requirements, customer reaction, financial priorities and corporate strategic posture. Enterprise structure changes often ensue.

Technological Change and Cost Management

Change in the business environment often triggers alterations in the structure and activities of enterprises including internal accounting and financial control systems. Change was relatively slow during the first half of the twentieth century because production technologies did not alter very rapidly. At the time, production processes in most large industrial enterprises tended toward the repetitive manufacturing of homogeneous products. Although investments in heavy machinery, which were essential to such processes, were high, the emphasis was on specialised production equipment for mass production which demanded repetitive labour manoeuvres. For each product produced, the relative machine cost input was very low but direct labour costs were high in proportion. This meant that calculations of full average costs per production unit of items had a relatively clear meaning since little distortion of cost prevailed given that most overhead costs could be allocated to large runs of relatively similar products.

Over the second half of the twentieth century, direct labour costs in manufacturing and service organizations declined in relation to total production costs. Starting from the 1970's in particular, many companies adopted flexible organizational technologies (FOTs), such as numerical control machines, just-in-time systems, computer-aided design and manufacturing approaches and other forms of flexible production technologies. The need for direct labour input diminished rapidly but by contrast, as investments were made into FOTs, overhead and support activity costs quickly expanded. This trend continues today as organizations invest in novel FOTs such as '3-D printing' and web-enabled technologies. The expansion in overhead costs arises not only from attendant depreciation, insurance and maintenance costs, but also from a new category of costs associated with servicing the new technology. Flexible forms of production technologies and digitised operating platforms within organizations require computer expertise, software updates, personnel training, scheduling systems and integrative information networking to link and coordinate automated production and processing activities. As a result, overhead costs can quickly rise just as direct labour costs continue to decline rapidly.

The growth in overhead costs intensifies with other enterprise changes also. The application of innovative work approaches, such as total quality management and just-in-time production systems, which seek to contain certain costs require additional overhead costs to be incurred. From the perspective of traditional costing logic, such changes in the manufacturing cost mix can be particularly problematic. Conventionally, direct labour served as the principal application base for indirect costs which tended to be low. However, where the overhead numerator grows at a pace not dissimilar to the swiftly diminishing direct labour denominator base, an inappropriately leveraged burden rate results:

| High overhead costs + Low direct labour input | = | Very high overhead application rate |

The demand for resources by different products is often not reflected accurately by a labour-based allocation rate within diversified production environments. During the 1980's and early 1990's firms began to revamp their costing systems to align them with the new complexities of organizational processes and production approaches. Many firms today are continuing on this path of costing system change given the shifting economics of technological and organizational advances that are on-going. This chapter considers the various techniques which have affected cost management practices in service and manufacturing environments.

The "New" Economics of Cost Management

In late 1995, a novel drive to capture further gains from technological advances began. The company Netscape Communications went public, signalling the beginning of the internet initial public offering (IPO) market. Its stock price doubled within a day as did those of e-Bay, Priceline.com, E*Trade among others undergoing IPOs. The value increases were reflective of the perceived potential of technological change by investors in companies which had no major products, nor profits or customers. This may lead you to ponder what constitutes technological change. For the purposes of this book, this is regarded as the recognition by an enterprise of new customer needs, existing customer needs that have not been met, newly emerging customer segments and new ways of manufacturing or distributing products and services. Of particular interest to us is that the nature and accelerated pace of technological change has raised issues concerning systems of cost management. This does not necessarily imply the irrelevance of past logic but a change in what is now regarded as relevant. Three trends are most apparent:

- Speed of operation has become a core competency for organizations. The ability to design and produce new products at breakneck speed has never been more important. Windows of opportunity for firms to develop and market new products have shrunk. Operational speed is of the essence in detracting competitors from reacting with a marketing offensive in the same product/service category in time. This is particularly so in markets where customers are known to have rapidly changing tastes and preferences. Speed of action does not however necessitate being first into an emerging market. Microsoft Explorer followed Netscape in the web browser market. Google is by far the most widely used internet search engine today, but entered the market after other search engine leaders such as Altavista. MySpace existed long before Facebook. But Facebook's uniform interface and simple look for pages enabled a more satisfactory user experience and allowed it to be an extremely successful second mover with about one in every seven people globally now using its platform.

- <u>Increasing returns to scale are possible.</u> Traditionally, industrialists regarded market systems as being based on scarcity – people made choices in the face of limited resources. Exchange economies find their roots in the idea that if an enterprise sells a product, ownership passes to the buyer. But exchange also takes place whereby an idea can be sold whilst it continues to be owned by the seller. In many industries, diminishing returns result as unit costs start to rise causing the gains from each additional sale to reduce. This is so if further structural investments are required to expand production capacity. Continued investments in production capacity lead to per unit cost containment. But as the extra capacity gets depleted, diminishing returns set in again at some point. In the past few years, we have witnessed business models where activity increases do not directly grow costs. <u>Information-based products</u>, such as books, music, software which can be digitised, are illustrative of increasing total returns with production. High fixed costs create virtually unlimited information goods production capacity. This is sometimes accompanied by very low variable costs enabling large-scale contribution from sales.
- <u>Fluid organizations are technology driven.</u> Strategic alliances between firms which may compete against one another are increasingly common. In a world of growing consumer sophistication and knowledge and of high product, technology and global complexity, firms realize that being good at everything is near-impossible. Strategic partnering enables firms to integrate different but complementary core competencies which can become a key competitive strength. Competitors share common goals which partnering can help achieve. Consider for instance the alliance created between Acxiom, a leading data mining firm and Accenture, a global management consulting firm. Acxion provides customer data which is embedded directly into Accenture's client-specific customer relationship management solutions. The alliance relies on technological interfacing bringing together core

competencies between two firms to create a unique client proposition.

Technological advances and the search for unique value propositions offer opportunities to firms willing to evolve away from traditional industrial structures. Sometimes, resulting entities have swiftly altering organizational structures which are so dynamic they can be considered fluid. Investments in internet technologies promote a new order of interfacing but also enable network-based interrelationships which redefine organizational boundaries – continuously. A growing number of firms are investing in social media technologies, collective intelligence systems, peer-to-peer networking, podcasts, wikis, blogs and mash-ups. Some commentators suggest that Web 3.0 technologies also change the economics of firm operations. Thus virtual blending of online and offline worlds such as browsing platforms which record user tastes and interests enabling web technologies to act as 'personal assistants' in their searches for products and services or in making recommendations. As noted in chapter 1, business analytics and 'big data' analysis enables an exponential increase in business intelligence. Some would suggest that this will be taken to the point where computers will be able to reason and analyze.

Emerging technologies can render less relevant traditional distinctions between price-makers and price-takers, consumers and product-designers, raw material provider and user, marketer and customer, product content and packaging, and product sale and consumption. The traditional conceptualisation of enterprise demarcations and boundaries do not apply to business entities such as Paypal, Skype, YouTube, Wikipedia and Facebook. In such commercial digital platforms which stress user-generated content, partnering can exist between firms as well as between product makers and product consumers. The forces of globalisation, technological digitization, and novel information exchange possibilities have altered traditional organizational structures and underlying income statement item connections. Companies can be freed from physical assets making them more flexible and fluid but rendering them also more uncertain and vulnerable. They can also pursue revenue gains without corresponding cost increases.

A company like Microsoft can enter and exit businesses like internet search, mapping, electronic payment, online advertising etc at a moment's notice – just as can any other enterprise. Disruption through constant organizational restructuring is a competitive move for many business entities. PayPal seeks to disrupt credit cards; Google seeks to disrupt information search boundaries; YouTube is disrupting television and opinion forming media; Spotify is disrupting music. Organizational fluidity is technology driven with technology no longer following strategy but co-existing with it.

Structuring altered strategies, financial controls and cost management approaches on the basis of new economic and business model philosophies necessitates different thinking approaches. Winterson (2000) illustrates the point by relating Gutenberg's experience with his apprentice: In 1439, Johann Gutenberg took an apprentice to help him produce a book on his new printing press. The apprentice was a forger by trade and was highly dexteritous and sharp-minded. Following a print run of Ovid's *Metamorphosis*, the apprentice asked Gutenberg how one might be able to tell which of the Ovids was the original. Gutenberg explained that the books were identical – any number could be produced – all original and all copies. The apprentice felt compromised thinking Gutenberg was taking him for a fool. The rule was there was always one original and afterwards copies and forgeries – that was how the market worked. Gutenberg persisted in explaining that all the books were equally valuable but equally worthless. This explanation angered the apprentice – to make his fortune Gutenberg had to stop telling his customers that he could print any number of Ovids. Gutenberg saw the value of his work in terms of abandoning the present for an altered future. The apprentice understood the invention within a rationality inherited from the past. In thinking about cost management activities, developing economic representations of the future potential of present-day activities rather than trying to visualise the financial consequences of activities in terms only of what is familiar is essential for modern enterprises engaging in strategic finance.

The traditional managerial logic of identifying the benefits that can be derived from economies of scale through mass production is, as noted above, changing as organizations implement FOTs, altered work organization methods and digitised business technologies. Firms now see merit in satisfying a greater diversity of customer needs by developing and producing a larger range of quality products and by providing custom-made products within a very short timeframe. Some enterprises use technologies to outsource product design to the customer. This is the basis of consumer based-content design sites. The adoption of flexible and digitised technologies to achieve novel goals is not necessarily a matter of choice. Rather, new methods of managing customer relationships, product diversity and multi-channel product offerings are sometimes the only strategic option a company can adopt in a highly dynamic and competitive market environment.

The adoption of altered production technologies, work organization approaches and digitised operating platforms rests on transformed philosophies about 'best' business practices. New managerial thinking is accompanied by product diversity, technological complexity and operational flexibility. One consequence of this is the reorientation of financial management practices for both operational activities and decision making. The rest of this section discusses technological and process related changes in the light of their implications for strategic finance practices. The starting point is a consideration of quality issues. After this, we discuss just-in-time systems, enterprise resource planning, computer aided and flexible manufacturing systems including 3-D printing and emerging e-business technologies.

Quality: What Is It and How Much Is Enough?

In competitive business environments, organizations need to ensure that high quality standards are achieved and that these change with time. Objectives for quality in many enterprises were formerly confined to product quality and therefore restricted to the shop floor where products were made. Quality concerns now embrace every function within organizations, from purchasing through to marketing and finance (Bendell et al, 1993). A focus on quality entails the following considerations:

Accepting that the only factor that really matters is the customer: if the customer is not happy with the product or service received then, by definition, there is room for improvement.

Recognising the all-pervasive nature of the customer/supplier relationship. Focusing on internal customers and satisfying their needs contributes to the final customer's satisfaction.

Moving from inspecting for conformance to a predefined level of quality to prevention of the cause of the defect in the first place.

Instead of an operator causing defects which are only recognised

'further down the line' after quality controllers have done their inspection, making each operator 'personally' responsible for defect-free production in their own domain.

Adopting zero defect programmes, in which an obsessive drive to produce things right first time is enforced. This is equally applicable to activities as diverse as raising a purchase order or generating the monthly management accounts, as to manufacturing defect-free components in the plant – or providing total quality satisfaction in the delivery of a service.

Deploying quality certification programmes are based on third-party audits of the extent to which a company can demonstrate that it has complete procedural control over all processes. If these are operating properly, they will result in the customer receiving the goods or services on time and to specification.

Emphasising the total cost of quality as a primary measure of all quality-related activities.

The above are considered relevant for any enterprise which attempts to manage quality of processes and organizational output. For any quality control endeavour, some notion of what constitutes quality is desirable. The quality of a product or service may be viewed as the totality of features which determine its <u>fitness for the use intended</u> by the customer. It is ultimately a function and a measure of customer satisfaction. It is also a reference to <u>conformance to the requirements</u>. These and many other views on quality exist.

> What is Quality?
> - "The pride of workmanship" (Deming)
> - "Conformance to Requirement" (Crosby)
> - "Fitness for use" (Juran)
> - "What the customer says it is" (Feigenbaum)

Often quality has to be regarded in terms that are very specific to the organization and its customers. If quality is seen to relate to fulfilling the customer's needs, and these needs include affordability, delivery at the right time, safety, reliability and after-sales support, then one may view quality costs as falling into one or other of two major classes. One category is that of the costs deliberately incurred in efforts to maintain or improve quality. This is called the <u>cost of conformance</u>. It includes the costs of both prevention and appraisal activities. The other category is that of the costs suffered as a result of bad quality. This is referred to as the <u>cost of non-conformance</u> and represents the failure costs. The former deals with what could go wrong, whilst the latter deals with what has gone wrong. Dale and Plunkett (1999) note that quality-related costs comprise both the voluntary costs of achieving a desired level of quality, and also the involuntary costs of failing to achieve it, i.e., the costs of conformance, and non-conformance (sometimes referred to as 'cost of quality' and 'cost of unquality').

The potential exists for quality management efforts to blend into existing and emerging cost management practices and thereby to integrate quality costing within internal financial control systems. In this respect, the Chartered Institute of Management Accountants define quality costs as:

> The expenditure incurred in defect prevention and appraisal activities and the losses due to internal and external failure

of a product or service through failure to meet agreed specification.

Figure 3.1 Categories of Quality Costs

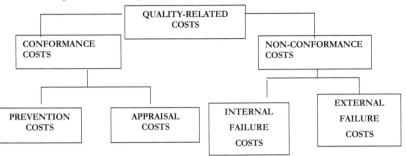

Each category of quality cost can thus be broken down into two further divisions as shown in Figure 3.1.

Cost of prevention refers to the cost of any action taken to investigate, prevent or reduce defects and failures. Prevention costs can include the cost of planning, setting up and maintaining the quality system.

Prevention costs are incurred to reduce failures and to keep appraisal costs to a minimum. They may include the following: quality planning; design and development of quality measuring and test equipment; quality review and verification of design; calibration and maintenance of quality measurement and test equipment; calibration and maintenance of production equipment used to measure quality; supplier assurance; quality training; quality auditing; acquisition, analysis and reporting of quality data; and quality improvement programmes.

Cost of appraisal refers to the cost of assessing the quality achieved. Appraisal costs can include the costs of inspecting, testing etc. carried out during and on completion of the product.

Appraisal costs are incurred in initially ascertaining the conformance of the product to quality requirements. They do not include costs from rework or re-inspection following failure. Appraisal costs may include: pre-production verification; receiving inspection; laboratory acceptance testing; inspection and testing; inspection and test equipment; materials consumed during inspection and testing; analysis and reporting of test and inspection results; field performance testing; approvals and endorsements; stock evaluation; and record storage.

Failure costs (internal) are the costs arising from within the organization of the failure to achieve the quality specified. The term can include the cost of scrap, rework and re-inspection, as well as consequential losses within the organization. Internal costs arise from inadequate quality discovered before the transfer of ownership from supplier to purchaser and external costs arise from inadequate quality discovered after transfer of ownership from the supplier to the purchaser. Internal failure costs may include the following: scrap; replacement, rework or repair; troubleshooting or defect/failure analysis; reinspection and retesting; fault of subcontractor; modification permits and concessions; downgrading; and downtime.

Failure costs (external) are the costs arising outside the organization from the failure to achieve the quality specified. The term can include the costs of claims against warranty, replacement and consequential losses of custom and goodwill.

A quality assurance department which is responsible for producing an estimate of quality-related costs might aim to involve the finance department in order to: prepare them for future responsibility for collecting the figures on a routine basis; produce figures which are valid within accepted limits of uncertainty with the objective of establishing the major areas of cost (which can then be re-examined if greater accuracy is needed); give some measure of the cost of quality and the savings potentially achievable; give a means of comparison between product and product, unit and unit, and possibly between the company and its competitors; give a base line against which future goals can be set and improvements measured; and propose actions to control and limit quality-related expense.

Some commonly useful sources of information for identifying and categorising quality costs are: payroll analyses; manufacturing expense reports; scrap reports; rework or rectification authorisations or reports; travel expense claims; product cost information; field repair, replacement and warranty cost reports; inspection and test records and material review records. The following additional sources can also be useful: organization charts; job descriptions; departmental budgets; standard costs at all stages of manufacture and standard or historic yields at all stages of manufacture. Measured costs of external failure can be based on data from sources such as: customer service department records of returns and replacements; legal department records of warranty claims and liability costs and failure analysis laboratory records of investigations and sources of fault.

When comparing quality costs in different plants, or on different occasions, one should attempt to make comparisons on a like basis. The particular ratio used will depend on the factor to be highlighted, e.g., quality costs in relation to labour utilisation, sales value, production costs etc. Some such ratios are: labour-based: internal failure costs/direct labour costs; cost-based: total failure costs/manufacturing costs; sales-based: total quality costs/net sales; unit-based: total quality costs/units of productions and added value-based: total quality costs/value added.

Organizations often find that if there is little or no investment in conformance costs, quality is likely to be poor: i.e., non-conformance costs will be high. Conversely, if more resources are invested in conformance activities, non-conformance costs will decrease and quality will improve. As quality improves, more difficulty will be encountered in producing further improvement.

Traditionally at the notional point where the conformance cost introduced is greater than the non-conformance cost it is intended to eliminate, improvement activity was seen to be uneconomic. Conceptually, there exists a point at which the sum of conformance and non-conformance costs is at a minimum. This has conventionally been seen as the optimal point of 'economic quality'. Producer and supplier at this point might accept the economic necessity for the incidence of defective items (see Figure 3.2).

It is to be noted however that quality must be defined broadly before it can be costed. One cannot assume that the loss from quality control should not exceed the intrinsic value of the rejected item. Suppose that a defective unit is installed in some medical instrumentation causing a heart pacemaker to have failed? Or that a failure caused the purchaser to find a different source of supply? Then, the loss of customer goodwill and product liability costs need to be considered. The costs of bad quality can far exceed the cost of good quality (Fargher and Morse, 1998).

Figure 3.2 Determining "Economic Quality"

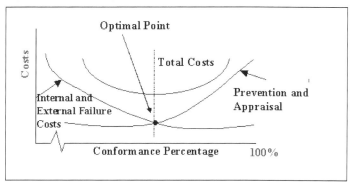

The traditional model ignores the time element. Preventive actions have no immediate impact on non-conformance, but typically, once they are in place they can reduce non-conformance costs throughout the market lifecycle of the product without further investment). Moreover, the argument subsumed in Figure 3.2 fails to differentiate between appraisal and prevention, or between internal and external failure costs. But appraisal and prevention have quite different effects on non-conformance costs. The traditional representation takes no account of changes occurring over the course of time. Consequently, it is preferable to plot the total cost of quality and its four components against time. An example is given in Figure 3.3. Such a plot allows improvements and setbacks to be made more visible. One can then ask: are our external failure costs being eliminated, since these represent quality as seen by the customer? Are our total failure (non-conformance) costs being reduced, since this represents our internal measure of quality? Are we reducing total quality-related costs by using prevention rather than appraisal?

Figure 3.3 Quality Costs Over Time

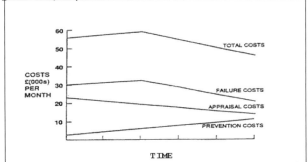

What underpins the philosophy that lack of quality can be more costly than ensuring its presence is the particular perspective taken on the management of quality. The conventional view of quality assumes that:

- Improving quality drives up time and costs.
- Defects and failures of less than 10% (typically) are acceptable.
- Quality should be inspected ex-post.
- Quality control should be a specialised and separate function.

The emerging view of quality considers that:

- Improving quality reduces time and costs.
- The goal is zero defects and failures.
- Quality should be designed and built-in.
- Quality control should be integral to production.

Customers and Quality

The modern view assumes that the total cost of quality incorporates the 'hidden' costs of quality. These hidden costs are included to recognise that they are often substantially greater than the traditionally measured failure costs. Hidden costs ultimately relate to customer satisfaction. They relate to externally perceived failures where the impact is easy to underestimate. Many factors are of relevance here, but customer satisfaction is perhaps the most important quality criterion. Figure 3.4 below depicts the potentially very high intangible external failure costs of not meeting customer expectations.

Figure 3.4 The Cost of Failure Can Be High

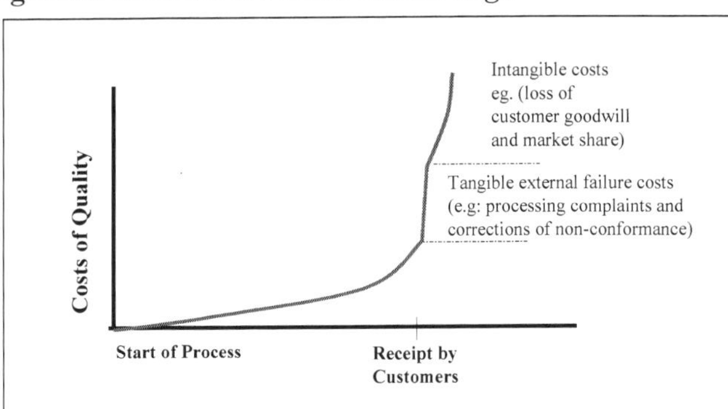

The modern conception of quality costs suggests that there is no economic quality point other than that where the product, service or process attains 100% quality conformance. In other words, costs are minimised only when optimal quality is generated (see Figure 3.5).

Figure 3.5 Modern Cost of Quality Concept

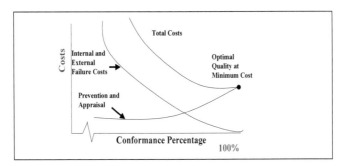

Enterprises that let their quality standards slip face major perception obstacles regaining customer trust. Consider Mercedes-Benz which suffered a major downturn in the quality and reliability ratings of Mercedes vehicles in the late 1990s and early 2000s. By mid-2005, Mercedes temporarily returned to the industry average for initial quality. But today – Mercedes-Benz according to some test drive results indicate continuing "Poor build quality" (see M. Darryl http://reviews.cnet.com/suv/2012-mercedes-benz-ml350/4864-10868_7-35089444.html) whilst others suggest the quality is improving. Similarly, Dell has been said to have been lax about the quality of its printers and laptops. One analyst writes: "Dell was able to achieve some savings through cost cuts a couple of years ago, but there's only so much more expense shaving that Dell can do now. Dell has a problem, and it's in the box" (see R. Munarriz http://www.dailyfinance.com/2012/05/24/why-dell-will-never-be-great-again/). Generally, perceived loss of product quality is difficult to remedy for any company. Customer who receive quality levels not in line with what they have paid for the products can be unforgiving (See www.ripoffreport.com and www.complaints.com).

Knowledge@Wharton report that many consumer goods multinationals have extended global markets by contracting out manufacturing to companies in China - mostly without letting quality standards slip. But Chinese firms often do not do this for home products: "Shaking off the shackles of low-quality manufacturing is a mammoth challenge for many." Perhaps given the 800 million low-income Chinese who accept poor quality for low prices, manufacturers may see it as okay to cut corners but the warning has been voiced: "When the majority becomes middle class, aware of quality and prefer quality to low prices, I think the Chinese market will change" predicts Kazuto Suzuki, a professor of international politics and economy at Hokkaido University (see: http://business.time.com/2012/03/23/china-makes-ipads-so-why-does-it-still-cut-corners-for-its-own-consumers/2/#ixzz1y3vYLbnA). McCall (2011) reports that only 15% of Chinese consumers in the cities of Beijing, Shanghai and Guangzhou feel that products made in China are excellent or very good whereas 44% hold this view of Japanese products (see Figure 3.6). The perception of good and bad quality can be ascribed to a nation rather than a specific company.

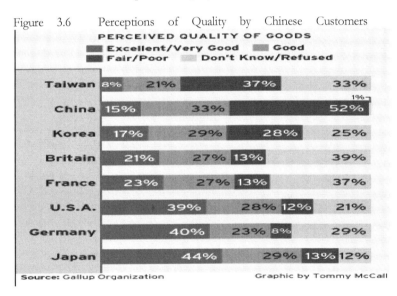

Figure 3.6   Perceptions of Quality by Chinese Customers

In the UK, quality related costs have been reported to range from 5 to 25 per cent of company turnover (Dale and Plunkett, 1999) and of this total 95 per cent may comprise the cost of appraisal and failure. The same is true of many North American firms (Evans and Lindsay, 2001). Consider a company which publicly admitted that its products were not perceived as being of high quality: General Motor's Vice Chairman, Robert Lutz, said that "A disturbingly high percentage of Americans have been programmed to believe that American cars in general – and GM cars specifically – are of terrible quality", (cited in Forbes Global 9.6.03. p.17). To counter this, GM sanctioned a corporate advertising campaign which emphasised that "30 years ago GM quality was the best in the world – 20 years ago, it wasn't". The campaign then detailed "the story of our long journey back". The relative lack of attention paid to quality issues in the US during the 1950-1970 period by many enterprises has been viewed as unfortunate. Whilst many North American management commentators advocated the prioritisation of quality by firms, their message was heeded by Japanese organizations more so than US ones. Figure 3.7 illustrates the consequences.

Figure 3.7: US Inc.'s Biggest Ever Mistake

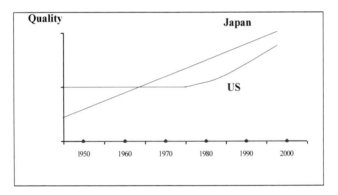

Making Cost of Quality Work

A linkage between a company's financial reporting system, the active involvement of accountants in total quality management (TQM) and the successful use of cost of quality (COQ) may be useful to identify in particular circumstances. Managers often understand the cost-benefit trade-off and use the economics of quality to assess the financial and strategic impact of a quality programme (Lynch, 1999). Companies like

Pilkington Glass and Xerox provide examples of the flexible use of cost definitions to show how reliable cost estimates of quality can make COQ a realistic gauge. These firms use COQ in their regular reporting scheme and link COQ to return on investment (ROI). They are examplars of how to evaluate key success factors that are deemed critical for product or service differentiation. Figure 3.8 shows a possible format for a COQ report.

Figure 3.8 An Example of a COQ Report

Category	Quantity	Allocation Rate	Total Cost	% of Sales
Prevention Costs:				
Design	No. of hours	£/hr	. . .	- -
Process Engineering	No. of hours	£/hr	. . .	- -
Appraisal Costs:				
Inspection	No. of hours	£/hr	. . .	- -
Internal Failure Costs				
Rework	No. of hours	£/hr	. . .	- -
External Failure Costs				
Customer Support	No. of visits	£/visit	. . .	- -
Warranty Repair	No. of repairs	£/repair	. . .	- -
Opportunity Cost of lost sales	No. of units	£/unit	. . .	- -
Total Cost of Quality			. . .	- -

Many companies, having successfully applied TQM principles in their plants, are beginning to realise its potential in other areas as well. Kalagnanam and Matsumura (1995) illustrate the use of COQ in a manufacturing company's domestic order entry department and the changes that resulted. They suggest that quality cost information can play an important role sensitising managers about making a commitment to quality. However, cost information can only be indicative of opportunities; it does not identify the problems or their sources.

Quality improvement requires information about the types of errors to investigate so that they enable the identification of sources of errors and the corrective action that may be taken. Quality costs information should not be used in isolation but only in conjunction with other measures of quality and productivity. Generating monthly cost of quality reports in isolation can be a wasteful exercise as far as quality improvement is concerned. The use of COQ numbers to evaluate managerial performance may lead managers to focus more on how to manipulate the numbers each month than on actually making improvements in the process. Inevitably, the deployment of quality costing imply consequent behavioural and organizational effects just as does any other financial control mechanism or cost management practice.

According to Carr (1995), COQ is simply a measurement tool that, when skilfully applied, can provide valuable insights into a company's quality efforts. But, there is little consensus today about the value of using COQ. Many companies use COQ calculations to arouse enthusiasm for a quality programme, only to quickly abandon the measure. Sometimes this occurs because of total quality related costs increase at the start of a quality programme since failure cost reductions tend to lag the incursion of voluntary quality costs. The organization seeing both conformance and non-conformance costs being very high during the initial phase of a quality management initiative may decide to abandon the effort just before the total costs start to show a reduction. This is depicted in Figure 3.9 below.

Figure 3.9 Giving Quality Time

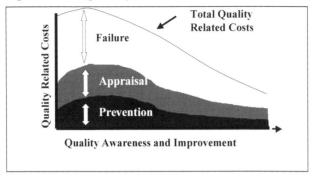

Many organizations have embarked on permanent quality improvement initiatives. They have used COQ successfully as part of their total quality management programme and regularly translate their quality efforts into monetary terms. There are two characteristics of successful and sustained use of cost of quality:

Financial managers are actively involved and help evaluate quality performance.

COQ is part of the overall management reporting scheme, which contributes to the acceptance and use of cost of quality information.

Despite the fact that managers regularly communicate using cost-based information, they often find economic definitions about quality inconsistent with their professional mindset or simply at odds with their cultural predisposition to thinking about organizational activities. The economics of business are often seen to be based on a knowledge and appreciation of costs. Costs may be regarded as useful in guiding finance trained managers' actions. But other managers may find operational measures, including statistical process control (SPC), to be good predictors and measures of quality. Figure 3.10 shows an SPC chart for tube production. The range of acceptable tube length tolerance is identified in the SPC chart. This range may be altered to reflect process changes. The statistics based visual depiction of quality and the operational as opposed to financial measures captured by the graph may be preferable for some managers to the presentation of similar information using financial metrics. Quality management programmes often must rely on the contextual preferences and management styles of individuals to achieve the desired intent.

Many companies pursue product or service quality because they believe it will improve their competitive position and, ultimately, their financial results. Some firms use quality as the prime competitive weapon for differentiating their products or service. The importance of quality has led to the development of measurement systems to quantify the pursuit of quality. These measurements aid in the management and control of the quality programme by providing managers an indication of the operation's success. Figure 3.11 shows how SPC can help establish parameters for tracking the achievement of quality improvement efforts. Reducing the allowable dispersion of process outcomes over time is illustrated here as being progressively achieved. To be meaningful, however, it has been argued that the measurement scheme must provide valued feedback and be a part of the management process of the organization.

Figure 3.10 Statistical Process Control

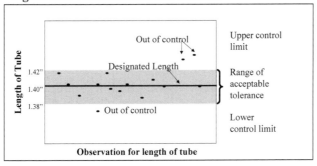

Most successful users of COQ deploy a range of quality-related performance indicators to enhance the value of the COQ measure. With the assistance of the finance function, managers can make the connection between product, process or service quality on the one hand and successful financial results on the other. They can monitor the costs and benefits of maintaining a given quality level for products or services. It is widely believed that good quality is synonymous with good earnings and return on investment (ROI). Companies like Xerox, Nestlé, Ford, General Electric, British Airways and Nokia have embraced this idea. Their adoption of quality as a central competitive methodology is considered to have produced enhanced corporate performance. Quality also continues to be viewed as a recurring theme in the management of many successful Asian companies.

Figure 3.11 Tracking Performance

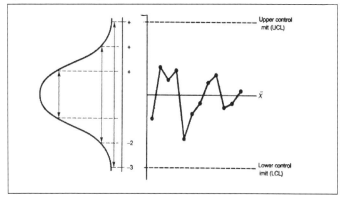

The flexible use of cost definitions and realistic estimates make COQ a possible surrogate performance measure of an organization's overall quality. When product or service quality is a key success factor, operating managers find that COQ can serve as an effective indicator of achievement, while also aiding in the selection of process improvement projects.

Managers often perceive the need to consider the indirect cost consequences of poor quality, including lost opportunities and lost sales. Where the costs of conformance can be reliably assessed, the costs of external failure can be less tangible but clearly very high. This realization often leads managers to invest presently to reap future benefits via reduced external failure costs. With the expansion of information technology, managers are often inundated with data. Every management effort may have its own possible set of associated metrics. COQ can serve as a useful management tool if managers can relate the format and data to the overall performance pursuits of the company. Quality is a factor that can contribute to the economic performance of an enterprise and which can be used to motivate managers to achieve highly relevant quality-linked organizational goals. But COQ has meaning and purpose to individuals

particularly when it shows congruence between quality programmes and a company's goals. COQ reporting can allow managers to generate commitment for quality projects and to link quality to economic returns.
Whilst COQ is a measurement tool that can assist in determining the impact of a company's quality efforts, it also acts as a potential indicator of process improvement and serves as a criterion for selecting projects to improve quality and return on assets (ROA). COQ can provide a link between economic performance and operational decisions. To successfully use COQ, financial managers need to become actively involved by helping to evaluate quality performance, and use COQ as part of the overall management reporting scheme. Quality managers often consider that quality needs to be framed in the language management best understands. Very often managers with a financial background, best understand money, costs and financial resources whereas marketing executives better visualize market share, product propositions and customer ratings. An alignment of the predisposition of managers toward data format and the nature of measures used to monitor quality efforts is always essential and typically highly organization specific. Chapter 5 further discusses integrated mechanisms for managing quality alongside other organizational concerns using the balanced scorecard and the quality function deployment approach.

Just-In-Time

Just-in-time (JIT) systems for guiding operational processes have been implemented by a wide array of enterprises. Just-in-time systems rest on a logic whereby production is initiated as a reaction to present demand. The systems in effect comprise two separate sets of activities:

JIT purchasing, which attempts to match the acquisition and receipt of material sufficiently closely with usage such that raw material stock is reduced to near-zero levels.

JIT production whereby production takes place only through a pull-system driven by the demand for finished products. Just-in-time production's aim is to obtain low-cost, high-quality and on time production by minimising stock levels between successive processes and therefore idle equipment, facilities and workers.

Some benefits of just-in-time purchasing include raw material stock reduction, control over delivery timing, close working relations with fewer suppliers, long-term contracts, quality assurance and raw material/subcomponent specifications. Just-in-time production, on the other hand, stresses work in progress and finished goods stock reductions, decreased lead and set-up times, zero defects, a flexible workforce, continuous improvement and quality control as part of the production process and producing to order. The underlying objective is for resources to be <u>pulled</u> rather than pushed through the organization (see Figure 3.12). Like total quality management effort, just-in-time systems emphasise the detection of production problems as they occur rather than establishing procedures for dealing with problems after production has taken place and setting aside facilities for further processing.

The <u>kanban</u> process can also support just-in-time production by acting as an information system through cards, which relay information about changes in type and quantity of inputs at different stages of production. Under kanban, a card is sent or signalled by a subsequent process to the preceding one when an item is withdrawn. Kanban connects all aspects in the flow of manufacturing within an organization through the provision of information about the category and quantity of materials going through the system by linking one process to the prior process. It can extend from vendors and subcontractors to the parent manufacturing firm.

> **A just-in-time system converts the structure of production into a process operation. Process costing methods may therefore be used to trace costs where production lines are treated as cost centres and unit costs are calculated by dividing costs of a period or an order over the units processed in that period. Direct labour may be treated as fixed and merged with overhead resources used in the form of period costs. Organization-wide cost pools may be abandoned in favour of activity-linked bases for allocating overheads (see chapter 4 on activity accounting). In this respect, just-in-time is appealing as it enables the identification of cost drivers by highlighting non-value-added activities. Price variances are often not necessary to determine given that long-term contractual links with suppliers exist. Performance evaluation under a just-in-time system is often different to a traditional <u>push-based approach</u> as actual rather than standard costs are stressed.**

Figure 3.12 The "Pull" Philosophy of Just-in-Time

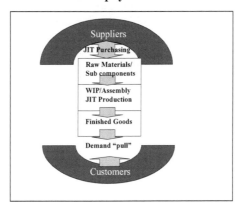

Variance analyses which tend to rely on static standards tend also to be changed as attention under JIT is directed towards material quality, supplier service, zero defects and throughput performance.

A just-in-time system enables more direct traceability of certain costs, which raises new possibilities for more comprehensive reporting. For instance, materials handling facilities are often dedicated to a single retail area or a single production line. Such operational costs can therefore be classified as direct costs of individual retail areas or production lines. In effect, many activities which previously would have been classified as indirect costs would, under just- in-time, be considered to be direct costs (see Table 3.1).

Table 3.1 Classification of Costs in Traditional and Just-In-Time Production Environments

Nature of Cost	**Traditional**	**Just-in-time**
Materials handling	Indirect	Direct
Repair and maintenance	Largely direct	Direct
Energy	Indirect	Direct
Operating supplies	Indirect	Direct
Supervision	Indirect	Direct
Production support services	Indirect	Largely direct
Depreciation	Indirect	Direct

Just In Case Or Just In Time?

Traditionally, the stock carried by an enterprise has been seen as having a trade-off between stock carrying costs and the costs of ordering. An organization may have expectations of production levels in line with its budgeted sales. This would indicate the number of subcomponents it will need the suppliers to deliver. The organization can minimize its ordering costs by ordering large quantities of the subcomponents infrequently and, thereby, stock the components in large quantities. Alternatively, it may choose to reduce the costs of carrying large quantities of stock by ordering much more frequently and thereby absorbing the consequently higher ordering costs. One might surmise that this trade-off will be indicative of a level of quantity to be ordered recurringly with defined frequency which will be lower in total cost terms to any other order level. Such a lower cost tallies with the <u>economic order quantity</u> (EOQ) to order (see Figure 3.13).

Figure 3.13 The Presumed Trade-Off

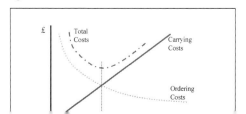

The following equation captures the two costs involved:

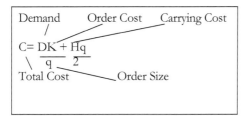

The rationale for the equation is evident given that D/q represents the number of orders which need to be placed and H/2 represents the notional average amount of stock carried over long periods of time. As such, if we assume that the yearly demand for subcomponents is 24,500 units, the ordering costs amount to £200 whenever an order is placed and the carrying costs are £5 per unit per year, then, since at the point of intersection of the two lines (see Figure 3.13), the costs of carrying the stock will be equal to that of ordering:

$$\frac{DK}{EOQ} = \frac{H}{2} x EOQ$$

Then,

$$EOQ = \sqrt{\frac{2.DK}{H}}$$

For our example,

$$EOQ = \sqrt{\frac{2 X 24500 X £200}{£5}} = £200 = 1400 \text{ units}$$

So whenever an order is placed, it would be for 1400 units. Each year 17.5 orders would have to be placed (one about every fourteen days assuming 245 business days per year). The total yearly costs incurred would be £7,000. The following graph depicts the flow of stock:

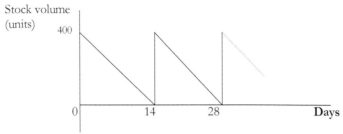

The enterprise may decide to hold an extra level of stock to counter uncertainties in the supply chain or to enable an unexpected surge in activity to be met. Naturally, the holding costs for the additional stock held (say 600 units as a <u>safety level</u>) would increase total costs:

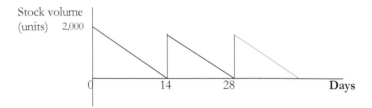

The main EOQ models assumptions are:
- Demand is constant and known
- Ordering costs are constant and known
- Carrying costs are constant and known
- Unlimited production and stock carrying capacity

As noted, where the total costs incurred are the lowest, the organization is assumed to have achieved the economic order quantity (EOQ). This represents the optimal quantity of stock to order whereby ordering and carrying costs are the lowest in total. But under the JIT approach, this presumed trade-off does not hold. This is because ordering costs can be minimized via long-term contracts with suppliers whilst the carrying costs are viewed as much higher than estimated because aside from the warehousing costs and the burden of working capital tied up in the stock, the stock itself may be subject to rapid obsolescence, changing customer tastes, substitute product development by competitors, etc. This suggests an EOQ of one unit which reinforces the JIT rationale.

Backflush Accounting

Any significant change in underlying operations is likely to justify a corresponding change in the accounting approach. The demand-pull emphasis on the physical flow of goods across the factory floor, which underlies just-in-time production, can be complemented by costs being determined retrospectively through a record-keeping technique called "backflushing". For just-in-time systems, backflush accounting has been regarded as a natural accounting consequence.

Just-in-time can allow accounting records to be simplified through backflush accounting whereby the level of detail with which product information is recorded is greatly reduced. A backflush costing system focuses first on the output of the organization and then works backwards when applying costs to units sold and to stock. In contrast, conventional product costing systems track costs through work in progress, beginning with the introduction of raw material into production. Backflushing focuses first on output and then works backwards when allocating costs between cost of goods sold (CGS) and stock with no separate accounting for work in progress (WIP).

Consider the JIT Company which manufactures scientific calculators and uses a backflush cost accounting system. The standard material cost per unit is £4.00 and the standard conversion cost (CC) is £3.00 per unit. Ten units are manufactured during its first month of operation and six units are sold. During the month £48.00 of raw material (RM) are purchased on credit.
Under a backflush accounting system, the point at which a sale occurs can be taken also to be the point at which accounting entries are made. Tables 3.2 and 3.3 depict the journal entries that would be made for the six units sold under a backflush system and a traditional cost accounting system respectively.

Table 3.2   JIT Co. Entries made under a Backflush

Accounting System

Cost of goods sold (6 units @ £7)   £42
    Conversion cost (6 units @ £3)   £18
    Creditors (6 units @ £4)   £24

The example above indicates the potential for cost reductions, which can result from using a simplified and less extensive accounting record-keeping system such as backflushing. The backflush entry for creditors (£24) of course does not reflect legal transfer of material and therefore ownership (£48). Thus, for final financial reports, an adjustment is still required. As it stands, the backflush entry accounts only for resource inputs for sales rather than full receipt of inputs from suppliers. A just-in-time system implies that physical material moves along the production line as sales are made rather than being pushed into production only to be stored in warehouses. Backflush accounting reflects the nature of this physical production flow by making accounting entries only as the demand-pulled production process takes place, thereby reducing book-keeping entries and their associated costs as shown in Table 3.3.

Table 3.3 JIT Co. Entries made under a Traditional Cost Accounting System

1. To record purchase of raw material on credit:

Material stock	£48	
Creditors		£48

2. To record the application of RM to work in progress for 10 units:

Work in progress (10 @ £4)	£40	
Material		£40

3. To record the application of conversion costs to WIP:

Work in progress (10 @ £3)	£30	
Conversion costs		£30

4. To record transfer of finished goods to warehouse:

Finished goods	£70	
Work in progress		£70

5. To record the sale of 6 units:

Cost of goods sold (6 units (£4 @ £3))	£42	
Finished goods		£42

Just as just-in-time generates new accounting needs, it also alters the costing system, making certain traditional practices redundant. For instance, an organization may ordinarily collect information on purchasing, warehouse and raw material inspection activities. These costs are subsequently placed into a cost pool along with others and a base such as warehouse space is used to allocate costs. Under just-in-time, long-term purchase contracts are used and the number of suppliers is typically reduced, thereby decreasing purchasing costs. Likewise, the goal of 'zero-stock' manufacturing eliminates warehouse storage requirements, and quality and quantity inspection procedures as well as working capital are greatly diminished. Such changes mean cost pools may alter considerably and allocation bases consequently have to be redefined.

Furthermore, under just-in-time purchasing, factors such as quality of raw materials, availability of subcomponents and reliability of supplies often take precedence over short-term price advantages. Price reductions of raw material and bought-in parts are often achieved by deploying long-term agreements with suppliers. Consequently, data on purchase price variances, which may have constituted an important part of accounting-based performance measures, lose relevance in a just-in-time environment. What is of essence is not to judge the performance of the purchasing manager as an isolated activity but to evaluate the production process as an integrated and complex set of interrelated functions. Likewise, recognising that just-in-time production entails a far-reaching form of decentralisation – whereby each individual factory worker can halt the production process when a problem arises, for instance - makes it doubtful that labour efficiency variance calculations offer much significance.

Performance evaluation indicators other than variances are affected by the application of just-in-time principles. Traditionally, the financial and cost management systems might report an array of monitors on a periodic basis, many of which are of little use given the growing importance of real-time information in enterprises today. Consequently, many firms report measures of managerial relevance regarding the achievement of quality objectives, reduction of stock, co-operation with vendors, on-time deliveries and process cost reduction. More specifically, measures including elapsed time, distance moved, space occupied and number of parts are used alongside metrics concerned with quality, cycle time and product complexity. Table 3.4 identifies some performance measures under traditional and just-in-time environments.

Table 3.4 Performance measures: Traditional vs Just-in-Time

Traditional	Just-in-time
Direct labour (efficiency, yields, productivity)	Total head count productivity
Machine utilization	Days of stock
Stock turnover	Group incentives
Cost variances	Customer service
Individual incentives	Knowledge-based factors

Enterprise Resource Planning

Just-in-time systems and quality management approaches can be viewed as work philosophies rather than technological advances. Conversely, enterprise resource planning (ERP) systems allow the integration and servicing of all the different functions of an organization by interlinking information bases. The precursor to ERP for many enterprises was materials requirement planning (MRP) which concerned itself with maximising efficiency in the timing of raw material orders placed with vendors and in scheduling the machining and assembly of the final manufacturing product. This made available components and sub-assembled parts just before they were needed by the next stage of production for dispatch. MRP systems were implemented as production and planning tools in traditional manufacturing contexts and entailed only a basic level of automation by way of computer software for back-scheduling production processes, in line with the required timing for delivering the final product to customers.

Early MRP systems depended on information based on weekly predictions, whereas later manufacturing resources planning (MRP II) systems, which linked medium- to long-term production plans with existing and planned capacities, needed daily updating. The objectives of MRP II systems included minimising stock levels, production run disruptions, storage costs and the extra expenses incurred in accepting rush orders. MRP II systems also provided forecasts of the production status of specific products and thus enabled the preparation of proforma statements for all categories of stocks by aggregating individual product forecasts. MRP II systems made evident the need to rate vendors on price, quality and delivery.

The original MRP systems emerged just as many larger firms made investments in mainframe computers. The time period 1950 to 1970 (Era I) was representative of this. But as organizations typically carried different functions across different departments, the information needs of these departments differed. Information processing was gradually becoming more sophisticated for activities such as product development, financial planning and working capital management, warehousing, marketing and manufacturing (Sandoe et al, 2001).

As organizations with functional structures moved into "Era II" (1970s and 1980s), the specific information processing needs of different departments could increasingly be met by the availability of personal computers. Mainframes were still the focus of some investments by organizations but not on the scale witnessed during Era I. MRPII systems gained popularity until around 1990. From 1990 to the present day, information technology management has progressed into a new era (Era III) with the emergence of the networked enterprise. Different information needs of different departments and functions can be met by enterprise integration whereby a single unified software approach with diverse modules achieves what was sought by the traditional standalone systems. As Koch (2003, p.7) notes:

Finance, manufacturing and the warehouse all still get their own software, except now the software is linked together so that someone in finance can look into the warehouse software to see if an order has been shipped.

Enterprise resource planning (ERP) systems enable such integration. An ERP system can take a customer order and provide a software road map which automates all the fulfilment processes in its path. A customer order can be linked to that customer's credit rating, order history, warehouse stock levels, transportation logistics, etc., via the ERP. These various "views" are accessible to any department that needs the information. ERPs are effectively software systems which enable the enterprise-wide integration of commercial and technical functions. ERP aims to provide instant access to data of all sorts generated by widely scattered and functionally diverse organizational and other sites. ERP systems' compatibility with digitised e-commerce business processes has greatly expanded over the past few years. Where software solutions traditionally specialised in accounting ledgers and related information processing, they now extend to human resources, marketing, manufacturing and distribution modules. At the core of ERP software, a central database (which may physically be distributed rather than really centralised) feeds data into modular applications that operate on a standard computing platform (Armstrong 2000). Business processes and data definitions are thus unified. ERP systems thereby provide consistency and transparency whilst making reliable and integrated information readily accessible in different formats. ERP solutions consequently cater for all the core formal information requirements of an organization.. ERP systems today enable the inclusion of a customer relationship management module thereby offering "front end" insight. This is useful to the sales task in that, for instance, a customer's "lifetime profitability" can be juxtaposed to the back end information to allow the organization to determine how far to allocate organizational resources to meet that customer's needs. In other words, the level of service provided to a customer can be calibrated in line with the resources this necessitates in the knowledge that economic gains will accord with the magnitude of value provision. Rather than just customising the product to the customer, the enterprise determines how far to customise the service to that individual customer. An ERP system can seek to make this possible through customer relationship management system linkages.

Naturally, ERP systems have objectives which may be highly organization-specific. But, in general, the following are common reasons as to why companies implement ERP. To:
- Integrate financial information;
- Standardize and speed-up manufacturing processes;
- Reduce inventory through better coordination and allocation of resources;
- Standardize human resources information;
- Integrate customer order information.

The cost of implementing ERP can be high. Koch (2003) reports on a study of 63 companies across diverse industries including small, medium and large firms. The total cost of ownership including hardware, software, professional services on internal staff costs over one implementation year and two subsequent years of maintenance, upgrade and optimisation range from US $400,000 to $300 million, with an average of $15 million. The study found that payback time was on average 31 months with median annual savings from new EPR systems being $1.6million. Another survey of 214 firms by IDC revealed that the adverse effects of business disruptions tied to ERP modifications can be very high leading to a 20.9% decline in stock price, a 14.3% revenue loss due to delayed product launches, and a 16.6% decline in customer satisfaction (http://panorama-consulting.com/ Vendors/IDC-2009Disruption-Survey.pdf). The survey respondents reported that making ERP changes ranged from $10 million to over $500 million. Whilst business change is fast and on-going, organizations must understand the potential cost and impact of business disruption tied to making current their ERP system.

Like many major organizational initiatives, ERP projects can result in budget overruns and other difficulties. The following are common underlying reasons:
- Training resource requirements can be very high;
- Extensive integration and testing is essential;
- Customizing the core ERP software to the business;
- Data conversion and analysis;
- Continuous need for consultancy;
- Training and then losing personnel
- ERP implementation may never stop;
- Post – ERP depression – the continuing incompatibility between the ethos of the system and the culture of the organization. Resistance to organizational change increases the likelihood of ERP system failure.

Vendors generally supplying the high-end and corporate marketplace have enthusiastically taken up the ERP approach. Organizations such as SAP and Oracle promote their products under the ERP banner. The need to supply an extended set of applications quickly has proven to be problematic for software suppliers. Some suppliers have extended their range of applications by writing the applications in-house, allowing them to provide a high-level of integration between their application areas. Certain organizations have chosen either to acquire or to form partnerships with other suppliers who have complementary software products.

Do ERP Systems Perform?

The adoption of integrated information systems in certain companies has suffered setbacks. In a survey conducted in 2012 by the Microsoft Dynamics U.S. Public Sector team in collaboration with the Government Finance Officers Association (GFOA) of 268 respondents, 75% reported that ERP implementation will – or did – fall short of expectations. Respondents thought a new system would cost anywhere from less than $500,000 to $10 million. In terms of software costs just over half of the organizations thought their expectations were met but only 38% in relation to implementation cost. Of the firms implementing new systems (rather than upgrading), 69% did not assess (or had plans to) assess ROI. (see
http://www.microsoft.com/industry/government/state/brightside/detailBlog.aspx?title=What_is_the_real_benefit_and_cost_of_an_ERP_system_GFOA_Survey_Reports_a_Mediocre_Experience).

It is important to clarify whether an ERP system extends an organization's existing practice or whether it is a departure into novel operational management terrain (Dechow, Granlund and Mouritsen, 2007; Granlund and Malmi, 2002; Scapens and Jazayeri, 2003). Whilst organizational level changes may be sought, finance and other managers are likely also to be affected by ERP systems implementations (Caglio, 2003). Some organizations have viewed business change in very narrow terms which is part of the problem. Simply altering the technology that underpins particular ways of doing business may be insufficient to reap anticipated potential benefits. Some commentators see it as important to develop an exploitation strategy relating to systems change as well as to pinpoint the desired benefits. Such benefits may entail financial analyses of relevant variables.

For most firms, the integration of information systems focuses on many business processes and cuts across many established functions. This necessitates an understanding of not just organizational processes and functions, but also of the organization's capacity for undergoing change. Determining the level of investment the enterprise makes in developing the requisite information design expertise and knowledge concerning systems integration issues will continue to grow in importance.

When the structure of information systems changes, conventional notions of effective control can become outmoded. Problems arise where systems retain the carcass of control priorities from the past. Thus, where ERP vendors attempt to create "end-to-end" solutions for an entire organization, control approaches will need to be revised. For instance, where new enterprise applications seek to enable seamless communication and interaction, control processes often rely on security checks and data flow stoppages. This may require the analysis and possibly a more extended restructuring of control systems for some companies.

Change is part of the environment in which enterprises operate and with the advent of web-based technologies companies will increasingly use the internet to link with their suppliers, trading partners and customers. Such changes are forcing a shift of emphasis from the internal focus typical of ERP systems to an increasingly externally oriented one. This enhances the importance of both business-to-business and front-office applications. Solutions which are more comprehensive than the structured logic of ERP systems may be required in the future. The outward orientation which is increasingly evident of business environments across the globe and which is buttressed by digital technologies underscores the potential relevance of thinking strategically about information systems investments. The strategic nature of financial systems which are concerned with external market factors alongside internal organizational processes are discussed later in the book.

Automation and Flexibility

Historians point back to 1495, when Leonardo da Vinci designed what is believed to be Western Civilization's first humanoid robot. But it would take until 1956 for the first industrial robot to be developed. The technology was invented by Joseph Engelberger – the "father of industrial robotics" – who convinced General Motors to finance and install the first industrial robot in 1961 at its Turnstedt plant in New Jersey. Today, over one million industrial robots are in operation of which two-thirds are located in Japanese factories and one sixth in North America (World Robotics 2011). The deployment of industrial robots is justified largely on economic grounds. This is set to increase given the continuously lower cost of computer components, improvement in vision systems and artificial intelligence software and flexible robotics systems that are more adaptable than their ancestors. As David Heilman, Chief Administrative

Officer at Seegrid – a leader in industrial automation notes: "Our customers are growing and innovating by using robots to increase facility productivity and efficiency to become more profitable, thus expanding their operations and adding more jobs. Robots are the high-tech tool companies are using to increase profits and grow their business." (see 18/5/2012   http://www.prlog.org/11877648-seegrid-industrial-robots-play-major-role-in-restoring-jobs.html).

Whilst hardware costs are decreasing and the range of functions achievable by any one machine is increasing, it becomes more important for software structures to be reconfigurable and enable robots to operate in environments with less structure. In other words, although robotics has long sought to enable a high level of flexibility, more often than not, when a robot completes one set of tasks, it needs to be reprogrammed to perform a different function. The cost of reprogramming can be very high. Thus flexibility is achieved by using many robots programmed to perform a small range of tasks. This is ideal for production activities that are largely predeterminable. However, the high fixed costs of deploying multiple robots is leading to researchers to develop more advanced robots which can reconfigure themselves and thereby operate in unstructured environments.

The use of robots in many automated environments assumes a high degree of integration with other manufacturing and organizational activities. For many years, customers, both industrial and retail-based consumers, have been able to use computer aided design technologies to customise products within pre-set parameters. Such computer generated designs (and sometimes computer aided tests) are sometimes linked to computer assisted manufacturing. This can entail the use of automated handling systems for subcomponents and stock flexible manufacturing systems which allow a high diversity of production possibilities and naturally, the utilization of robots. These various computer-based flexible organizational technologies and their cost management implications are considered below.

Computer-Aided Design and Computer-Aided Manufacturing

Computer-aided design and computer-aided manufacturing (CAD/CAM) refers to a blending of mechanical and computer technology to facilitate the designing and manufacturing of a product. CAD/CAM systems can potentially take an engineer's vision of a new product from the idea phase to actual product in a fraction of the time required previously. Specifically, computer-aided design entails the use of computers in the course of developing, analysing and modifying the design for a product. A typical system capable of performing the tasks required includes hardware elements such as computer, keyboards and graphics monitors. The software required includes a graphics package and the applications programs. Computer-aided manufacturing refers to the use of computers to plan, implement and control the production of a product through the utilisation of manufacturing facilities and resources. Such systems range from those that generate plans that people must implement and control to those that develop the manufacturing plans and implement and control the operations according to those plans while, at the same time, reacting to variations between planned and actual performance.

The decision to use CAD/CAM technology is difficult to analyse using conventional financial capital appraisal techniques because of the wide array of intangible benefits which are not easy to quantify (for instance, improved design drafts, better customer perception of products, increased productivity of draughtsmen and enhanced product quality). Cost control in CAD/CAM settings is also problematic because of the difficulty of setting labour standards for activities such as drafting and design. Moreover, with experience, these activities result in increased productivity and reduced operational time which generates the need to continuously update standards. Product costing is simplified when engineering and design costs can be ascribed to the production of a specific order. Performance measures can be tied to improving set-up times, materials usage and manufacturing time, defect rates, product versatility and quality for which no simple measures exist but where there is a need for customization for different production contexts.

Flexible and Computer-Integrated Manufacturing Systems

A flexible manufacturing system (FMS) refers to a computer-controlled production system intended to produce a family of parts. In an FMS, workpieces of different types travel between and are processed at various programmable, multi-purpose machine tools and other workstations. Parts flow through the system according to individual processing and production requirements. A number of companies utilise computer-controlled FMSs running unattended on night-shift operations.

Production technologies such as CAD, CAM and robots are used to partially computerise factory environments so that FMSs contribute to islands of automation (IA) buffered by intermediate storage of semi-finished/assembly products. IAs can be integrated so as to automate fully the production process under total computer integrated manufacturing (CIM). The main advantages of an FMS over a traditional factory organization structure include the ability to produce differing varieties and volume levels using the same technology, quick customer response, and reduced labour costs as materials-handling systems and automated storage and retrieval systems replace labour. In addition, there are savings from the actual automation of manufacturing processes which themselves cut down on human operators. Where industrial robots are used, there is a clear reduction in labour costs, minimization of errors with workers freed from having to perform dangerous or merely repetitive tasks.

The use of robots during the 1990's was problematic to the extent that a minor adaptation in production required taking a robot cell or group of robots carrying out specific tasks offline which was very disruptive. But today, offline software applications permit engineers to programme robots and to make adjustments remotely without disrupting production. This means that designing and bringing a new product to the market takes less time. Whereas it used to take manufacturers four to seven years from design to production to bring a car to market, with advances in software applications, companies like Toyota are attempting to cut the product life cycle to one year. The advent of flexible manufacturing systems whereby technology gains in robotics hardware and software applications are integrated has led firms to leverage this as a core competitive advantage. The ability to remotely and dynamically orchestrate many aspects of design and production using computers, including gathering real-time data on manufacturing processes and distributing it over the internet to various links in the supply chains (see chapter 5), provides some enterprises with a strategic edge. Broadly, product quality, set-up times, machine utilisation, low stock levels, space and enhanced information on production are all affected favourably by automated production in technologies such as FMS. It is impossible to quantify all such benefits, which makes it difficult to justify FMS expenditures in purely financial terms.

Cost control, product costing and performance measurement problems arise principally from the reduction in indirect labour utilisation and the high capital cost components of an FMS. Consider the tyre industry where vertical integration has been maintained by the major companies. Rather than outsource, tyre makers like Goodyear, Michelin and Bridgestone tend to build their products from scratch starting with latex rubber from plantations to the production of wire and fabric around which rubber is wound as well as the in-house design of moulds which define each tyre's outer contours. The implementation of flexible organizational technologies in this context differs widely from that within motorcar companies which can focus on assembly and engage heavily in outsourcing.

The economics driving investments in tyremaking differ from those of the automaker. The focus traditionally was on machine yield rather than worker productivity. Presently, increasing raw material prices and a decreased tolerance for premium prices in spite of more complex tyre designs has altered the financial basis of FOT investments. A tyre is increasingly being seen as a commodity rather than a differentiated product. The ability to achieve mass customisation is becoming crucial in the industry in an attempt to command premium prices but as one tyre analyst has noted: "You can talk about performance all you want, but it's a piece of rubber" (Chiara Tirboni cited in Fortune 28.5.2001, p.86). The changing nature of the industry brings with it financial, operational and strategic issues to consider. Investment appraisal becomes complex. Pirelli for instance, has invested over £60 million in a robot based production line which can build a new tyre in three minutes without human hands and in a fraction of the space of a conventional tyre making facility. Likewise, Goodyear is investing in a similar multimillion dollar system referred to as FMS II which is expected to be totally automated with no workers and which will be able to switch production swiftly between different types of tyres. Evaluating such an investment in financial terms is complex as many risks and uncertainties have to be assessed.

Often FMS entail the use of <u>material handling systems</u> (MHS) which move stock within and between manufacturing, assembly or shipping functions. The systems are characterised primarily by manual operations for moving the stock to, within and from the storage area, and the handling of paperwork to keep track of stock quantities and locations. These systems have in many firms been replaced by <u>automatic storage/retrieval systems</u> (AS/RS) which store and receive parts and products and which can be integrated into a computerised manufacturing operation to keep accurate track of stock and deliver required parts at just the right moment. AS/RS systems increase the speed and accuracy of stock storage and retrieval in the automated factory.

In such dynamic market environments where advances in technology, altering product features, changing consumer expectations and transformed resource deployment are prevalent, decision-makers become concerned about the growing complexities of product costing and capital budget analysis. These are reflective of issues which effective cost management systems need to address:

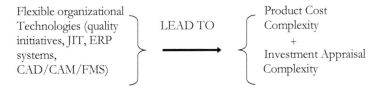

Some manufacturing organizations have attempted to invest in totally computer integrated manufacturing operations which use negligible levels of labour resources in relation to total plant investment. Such facilities offer a level of technological flexibility that is essential in product markets characterised by extremely short product life cycles. Moreover, they may provide the necessary capability to alter and perhaps extend product life cycles which may be a core strategy for survival. In such contexts, market opportunities permitting desired levels of profitability may be of short duration. Developing appropriate strategic financial management expertise to recognise such market opportunities quickly and to mobilise manufacturing design and production correspondingly is becoming part of organizations' essential core strengths. Production technologies which permit flexibility across corporated web-based systems, places enhanced pressure on organizations to understand and manage costs across business-to-business boundaries. Such changes are influencing the design of financial management systems in organizations across many industries.

Additive Manufacturing

Additive manufacturing refers to the production of three dimensional solid objects from digital data files. Also referred to as 3D printing, it is undertaken by adding layers successively on existing layers of material rather than starting with material from which material is subtracted via boring, milling, grinding, sanding etc. Additive manufacturing is undertaken via computers hooked up to 3D printers. This has opened up a fast growing market for the production of 3D printing machines over the past few years. Many different products can be manufactured in this way including automotive parts, shoes, jewelry, ornaments, dental and medical products and information systems elements. The range of industries affected by additive manufacturing is growing.

The 3D printing process works with data from a CAD drawing being fed into a printer. Successive layers of liquid, sheet material, powders are laid one on top of the other to build up a model which are later fused together to achieve the final desired structure. The additive nature of the process reduces traditional costs of wastage and defects.

One company which uses 3D printing is Shapeways which was started in Holland but later established its head office in New York. The company engages an online community of producers/inventors who contribute to the final digital prototype alongside input from Shapeways. The company ships over three quarters of a million products. A user can upload a design and obtain a quote for the printing with a choice of different materials. Shapeways provides a sales platform also to sell the items produced.

The model has important implications according to Peter Weijmarshausen, Shapeways' chief executive: "The first is speed to market: Shapeways had covers for iPads on sale just four days after Apple first launched the device in 2010. Second, the risk of going to market falls to almost zero because entrepreneurs can test ideas before scaling up and tweak the designs in response to feedback from buyers.

Some Shapeways products go through 20-30 iterations a year. And third, it becomes possible to produce things that cannot be made in other ways, usually because they are too intricate to be machined." (cited in "All together now:The advantages of crowdsourcing" The Economist,21/4/ 2012).

Another New York based company Quirky specializes in product-development to make prototypes of products which are collaboratively synthesized. Under this model, users submit ideas online and can be involved at all stages including final design, packaging, marketing and pricing. For a range of product ideas with potential, Quirky will identify the right manufacturers with the product being sold on the Quirky website and sometimes external retailers. The company assumes responsibility for patents and standards approvals. It will share the revenues with the inventors and those who collaborated in the manufacture.

Additive manufacturing has cost management implications. It requires relatively small capital for machinery investment; it can rely on a community of inventors removing the need for a firm to invest in costly product innovation staff; it can overcome problems of high labour costs in the developed world for repetitive tasks thereby reducing the labour cost differentials between different parts of the world which drive many manufacturing location decisions; manufacturing can take place 'on demand' where production is swift which reduces many stock control and storage costs; economies of scale effects are not appreciable so small producers are not disadvantaged relative to high volume producers; mass customization can be readily effected with 3D printing acting on direct and swift digital specifications input; A 3D printer can 'print' a product as a complete part with no assembly required and it can produce mechanical items with some moving parts – reducing product breakdown often caused by assembly; the additive nature of the process reduce material costs tied up in waste and with a lesser need for a variety of material/sub-component supplies which need storing, security, environmental controls etc; and digital files containing detailed specifications remove the need for high cost specialist personnel.

If a manufacturer was asked to produce one single screwdriver to a unique set of specifications, it would require a mould to be made, the head to be casted, a suitable machine finish to be achieved, and different parts to be assembled. The pricing would reflect this and the screwdriver would be priced at a prohibitively high level. The process would be economically viable only if a large volume was produced to spread the fixed costs and take advantage of economies of scale in production. In a 3D printing environment, the economies of scale are much less important. The cost of setting up the printer does not alter the cost of the individual units produced to any great extent. This renders manufacturing of a single customized item much cheaper than with traditional manufacturing infrastructures. In addition to this, additive manufacturing enables different elements of the product to be made in one go rather than being riveted together from other individual sub-components. The lesser use of sub-components reduces costs both of assembly as well as those of ordering, tracking, storing, moving and processing these sub-components. The digitisation of manufacturing allows things to be made to design, more economically and more flexibly with lesser labour input.

These and other cost implications associated with additive manufacturing enable manufacturing innovations in both product and new business models. It is likely that in the near term, economies in the developed and developing world will see increased use of digitized manufacturing technologies with attendant financial implications.

Creating Fluid Organizations

As noted above, operational techniques and technologies have altered in the production and provision of services. Enterprises continuously innovate products, production techniques and ways in which they compete in increasingly intense markets subject to globalizing forces and effects. Many firms opt for cost leadership in their product types whereas others choose to differentiate their product offerings from other competing firms sufficiently to earn premium prices. Many enterprises seek to do both. Some enterprises with product offerings which cannot sustain differentiation over sufficiently long periods of time because of swift replication by other market incumbents find that their products lose their characterising elements and become commoditized rapidly. Where competitive strength becomes less sustainable through product characteristics, some firms opt to differentiate their design and structure more so than their products. Firms within industries opt for different design strategies. Examples are Adidas vs Nike, Tesco vs Wal-Mart, Zara vs Gap, and HP vs Dell. These firms' products find many non-brand parallels but adopt highly different internal structuring approaches. The advent of digital technologies and globalization forces enhance firms' potential to achieve this.

It has been argued that organizational re-design can be resource intense but its returns in profits, costs and risks often surpass investments in product design and other strategic initiatives (Bryan and Joyce, 2007). Building strategy via organizational designs is an evolutionary step departing from the firm structures of the twentieth century industrial era when capital, labour and land were the scarce resource and vertical hierarchical structure and extensive expertise focused managerial hierarchies were regarded as fundamental to efficient performance.

By shifting the organization so as to mobilize the intellectual capital of the workforce and tap into its knowledge, relationships, and skills capacities, firms are finding that they can create sources of significant new wealth at relatively low risk. Modernizing organizational designs can trump the gains generated by other, more traditional strategic initiatives.

As organizations become firmly ensconced in knowledge economies, the creation of wealth can be achieved via a new focus: maximizing returns on people instead of just on capital. This translates into creating organizations that can continuously adapt and re-evolve instantaneously. Effectively, traditional structures are giving way to fluid enterprise designs.

Bryan and Joyce (2007) note that: "Today's companies must redesign themselves to remove unproductive complexity while simultaneously stimulating the effective, efficient creation and exchange of valuable intangibles. They must be able to mobilize mind power as well as labor and capital." In today's digital and global economy, many historic trade-offs lack no longer retain significance. Thus interaction and transaction costs which have tumbled lead to the idea that what matters is no longer whether hierarchy or collaboration is better. Hierarchy and collaboration are essential aspects of all large, successful enterprises. The critical issue for performance-focused enterprises is how to mobilize intellectual resources whilst removing ineffectual complexity.

4

MAKING ACTIVITIES PROFITABLE

A unit of Dutch giant ING, ING Direct offers low-maintenance customers with high interest rates on savings accounts and low interest home equity loans among a handful of other products. The bank has been said to "fire" about 0.18% of its customers every year according to its CEO. Ditching clients who are too time-consuming saves the company at least $1 million annually. ING Direct has driven its cost per account to a third of the industry average. Many service-based enterprises undertake analyses of individual product and customer costs to understand how profits are driven at the micro-level. First Chicago Corporation, a part of Bank One, prepared income statements for every client, and applied a 'teller fee' on some of the money-losing customers. About 3% of the bank's clients closed their accounts. A proportion of customers became more profitable via increases in their account balances to avoid the fee or by visiting cash machines instead of the tellers. First Chicago lost some customers but improved the profitability of most. Understanding the costs of customer service and other activities which drive costs has made cost management a core element of competition in many enterprises.

Changing Standards

An understanding of costs is considered fundamental to many aspects of management because if they are not controlled, an organization may risk becoming unprofitable and imperilling its existence. The management of costs is invariably challenging because notions of costs are always context dependent. Costs can only be expressed within a set of rules, conventions or ideals – there is no universally applicable conception of an "absolute" or "true" cost. Different managers have differing ideas of what costs what and what should be costed. These differences have become more apparent as uncertainty and complexity in business environments have grown. The field of financial management has seen more calls for change in the past twenty five years than it has in the whole of its prior history. The rise of new management philosophies, alterations to work organization approaches, the implementation of more flexible organizational and digital technologies and a fast altering global business environment are factors that have led to reforms being advocated. Today, well established financial management tools continue to be used by many companies. But also, novel management techniques are being adopted as new enterprise management situations emerge.

Accounting for costs has evolved over the course of the twentieth century under the principal concepts of job costing, standard costing, activity-based costing and strategic cost analysis. During the early part of the twentieth century, material and labour costs within manufacturing concerns were recorded for each unit of production. Overheads were ordinarily allocated to produced units. Cost determinations used in production were generally kept simple as this reflected the tracking of simple economic flows across the enterprise. Standard costs have from this time reflected perceptions of optimum or ideal cost of materials and labour required in production. Overhead costs have also been tied to products or services on the basis of direct labour or machine hours applied. Actual costs measured against pre-determined cost standards and variances have been investigated with deviations from expectations being analysed to usefully contribute to managerial decisions.

The use of standard costs for material, labour and overhead resources today find wide usage in modern organizations. Standard costing is most commonly used in industries where there are many identical units of production – for example, automotive components or white goods. It can also be applied to service industries such as banking and insurance where the performance of certain tasks is very repetitive. Many manufacturing companies rely on standard costing for the valuation of stock. A focal element of standard cost systems traditionally has been the recognition of resource usage as varying principally with the scale of output. Scope effects have not been of primary concern to firms whose productive output can be characterised as relatively homogeneous.

Although the basic tenets of activity analysis have been applied as a matter of convention in some companies since the 1920s, a reformulation of its logic was publicised extensively in the early 1980s. This was in some instances presented as an alternative to conventional methods of overhead apportionment. Many companies which have carried out activity-based cost analyses by more explicitly incorporating scope effects into their costings, consider the exercise as having been valuable in providing a new perspective on product costing and as a basis for efficiency gains. Some of these companies have implemented <u>activity-based costing</u> (ABC) systems for day-to-day cost monitoring or stock valuation capturing both scale and scope effects.

The ABC Phenomenon

ABC entails the examination of activities across the entire chain of value-adding organizational processes underlying causes of cost. It attempts to overcome cost distortions by addressing cost behaviour parameters, which include <u>non-volume cost drivers</u> reflective of production complexity and product diversity in addition to <u>volume-linked drivers of cost</u>. Although one output of ABC calculations is cost information based on resource consumption, the actual process of deriving such costs offers a number of monitors which may be useful for a variety of managerial purposes. These include novel performance measures, altered budgeting techniques and a large amount of decision-making information tied to the broader concept of activity-based management. <u>Activity accounting</u> is often used to refer to activity-based costing, activity-based management (ABM) and their variants. ABC continues to influence costing practices across a very large number enterprises globally. The image of accountants has been said to have continually altered from being "numbers technicians" to being contributors to managerial insight and action with the introduction of strategic tools like ABC and ABM.

What Drives Costs?

During the first half of the twentieth century, production processes in most European and North American enterprises tended to be geared toward the repetitive manufacturing of homogeneous products. High direct labour costs constituted a significant portion of direct costs which vary directly with production output. As such, little cost distortion was introduced when manufacturing overheads were allocated across a portfolio of relatively similar products.

During the second half of the twentieth century, direct labour costs in manufacturing organizations declined in relation to total production costs. As companies adopted flexible organizational technologies such as computer-aided design, robots, flexible manufacturing systems and other forms of automated production technologies, the level of direct labour input diminished rapidly. Likewise as enterprises invested in automated technology, overhead costs and support activities quickly grew. This was not only caused by growing depreciation, insurance and maintenance costs, but by a new category of expenses associated with servicing the new technology, which necessitated additional indirect support resources. Flexible forms of organizational technologies ordinarily require computer expertise, software updates, personnel training, scheduling systems and integrative information systems to link and coordinate automated production activities. As a result, overhead costs can quickly rise. It is the very use of the resources adopted which cause the overhead increases that also causes direct labour cost input decreases.

The growth in overhead costs intensifies with the application of innovative work approaches such as total quality management and just-in-time production systems, which help contain certain costs but which may require additional overhead cost incursion. Further, additive manufacturing, although in its infancy, will alter overhead cost control in firms too. Whilst small in terms of current manufacturing output, additive manufacturing or 3D printing machines that build layers to create three-dimensional solid objects from digital specifications are changing the economics of production. Prior to 3D printers, firms had to create their own prototypes which consumed time and resources and often required skilled craftsmen or expert engineering input. But with the advent of such technology, prototypes can be insourced and modified if required which alters drastically the configuration of cost drivers. Cost management systems are having to react to these cost structure changes which impact profitability and corporate performance.

Many firms consider that there may be considerable merit in satisfying a greater diversity of customer needs by developing and producing a large range of quality products and perhaps even by providing custom-made products within minimal timeframes. Product diversity is sometimes the principal strategic option perceived to be open to a company operating in a dynamic and competitive market environment. Using FOTs to achieve this as noted will increase overhead costs and decrease labour cost input.

The rise of innovative business models adopted by internet companies is also a way to provide different products with reduced direct cost inputs. Here the potential for similar cost distortion arises. But additionally, the revenues generated by the firm will not be closely tied to the costs of providing the service to the users. This is yet another source of cost allocation concern as the pricing of the product will not directly tie-in to the cost of the product to the users.

In modern firm contexts we thus find that overhead costs increase and direct resource input reduction takes place concurrently. For firms that use traditional costing approaches, such types of changes in the cost mix can be quite problematic. Generally, where the overhead numerator grows quickly and is accompanied with a rapidly diminishing direct labour denominator base, an inappropriately high leveraged burden rate results. This can make a simple overhead allocation system inappropriate because the growth in costs incurred will not be a direct reflection of the volume of output produced.

The Logic of Activity Analysis

Empirical studies of organizational costing practices suggest that many firms have attempted to achieve profitability by managing costs which do not necessarily reflect resource-consuming activities. Costs are reported on the basis of responsible organizational units and in terms of production activities rather than as representing, in accounting terms, the utilisation of resources by organizational processes. Using cost as a substitute for activity does not pose any difficulty where the manufacturing process is relatively simple and produces homogeneous products. Here, production costs may be readily traced and allocated to produced units. This is the traditional approach to costing (see Figure 4.1).

Figure 4.1 Traditional Product Costing

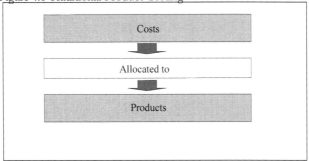

In more sophisticated organizational environments however, product quality, diversity and complexity are viewed as critical in maintaining competitiveness and dictating how resources are used. In these contexts, activity-accounting information can be much more useful than traditional costing data, as it sets out to capture cost causality factors in a more transparent manner. Accordingly, The Chartered Institute of Management Accountants (CIMA, 2000) defines ABC as 'an approach to the costing and monitoring of activities which involves tracing resource consumption and costing final outputs. Resources are assigned to activities and activities to cost objects based on consumption estimates. The latter utilise cost drivers to attach activity costs to outputs'.

Activity-based management produces information that goes beyond costing and monitoring pursuits by focusing employee efforts on continuously improving quality, time, service, cost, flexibility and profitability. In this light, CIMA defines activity-based management as a 'system of management which uses activity-based cost information for a variety of purposes including cost reduction, cost modelling and customer profitability analysis' (CIMA, 2000).

A guiding principle of all ABC systems is the view that the organization is made up of activities: activities consume resources and cost objects (usually products) consume activities. This is in contrast to traditional accounting, where costs are consumed by cost objects (mainly products). With ABC, the focus is not on the amount of each type of general ledger costs, such as wages, equipment, power and supervision, incurred by a department, but on the costs of the activities undertaken in the department. Thus, the conventional costs of a department would be via the activities carried out to the department.

Activity-based information may be non-financial or of a strategic cost nature. It can include any relevant data about activities across the entire chain of value-adding organizational processes, including design, engineering, sourcing, production, distribution, marketing and after-sales service. Information of this kind focuses managers' attention on the underlying causes (drivers) of cost and profit on the premise that individuals cannot manage costs but they can manage activities which cause costs to be incurred.

The manufacture of a product entails many processes which add cost to the product, but not all such activities necessarily add value to the product. It is therefore possible, in principle, to differentiate between <u>value-added</u> and <u>non-value added</u> activities, according to whether or not the elimination of an activity from the operational process would result in a deterioration of product attributes such as performance, function, quality and perceived value, and thus reduce the value perceived by the customer. This is shown in Figure 4.2 below.

Figure 4.2 Adding Value across the Value Chain

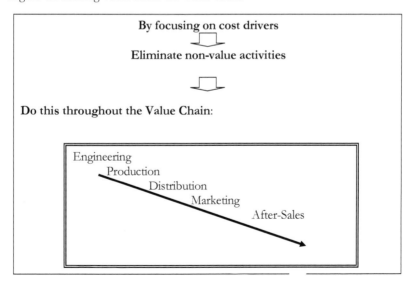

Production approaches such as just-in-time systems, flexible manufacturing systems and enterprise resource planning solutions place emphasis on eliminating waste, delay, excess and unevenness of product whilst integrating information relating to functional and auxiliary processes. It is potentially useful for managers to attempt to identify activities that waste organizational resources since they do not augment the customer's perception of a product's value. Such a perspective highlights a key objective of activity accounting systems which is that in re-thinking costing, the organization is exposed to costs which can be eliminated without damaging the value of the product or service to the customer.

Scope versus scale

Problems may arise where traditional cost accounting systems, designed to value stock for financial reporting purposes, are assumed to provide a measure of the organizational resources used up in their production. One reason for this is that overhead cost growth can be due to increased diversity (or scope) of output rather than the volume (or scale) of output. A traditional cost accounting system which allocates overhead on the basis of scale of output rather than scope of output will tend to <u>overcost</u> high volume products and <u>undercost</u> low volume products (see Figure 4.2)

Figure 4.3 What Causes of Cross Subsidization?

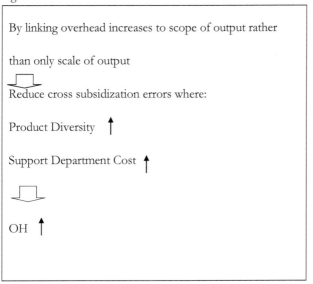

Where there is cross-subsidization between products, the distorted cost information can encourage managers to proliferate low volume complex product lines which may, indeed, be loss-makers even though they may seem profitable under conventional accounting reports. Accompanying this managerial decision may be the further decision to drop high volume product lines which may appear unprofitable. As Cooper (1987, p. 219) explain:

Low volume products create more transactions per unit manufactured than their high volume counterparts. The per unit share of these costs should therefore be higher for the low volume products. But when volume related bases are used to allocate support-department costs, high volume and low volume products are not treated differently because each individual unit produced represents the same volume of production ... high volume products receive an excessively high fraction of support-department costs and, therefore, subsidise the low volume products.

Most cost systems in manufacturing firms use a <u>two-stage cost-tracing</u> procedure for non-direct costs, whereby the first stage assigns resources to specific segments of the production process (departments). The second stage traces costs to products by using some measure of the quantity of resources consumed by each product. It is the choice of overhead application measure in this second stage which is seen as being able to distort costs if it is not chosen carefully. As noted above, the risk is that products produced in large volumes get assigned more than a proportionate share of resource costs. The beneficiary products or services are those which are produced in low numbers (see Figure 4.4).

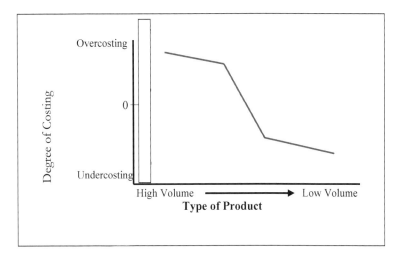

FIGURE 4.4 Costing Accuracy versus Volume

Long-term versus Short-term Cost Behaviour

Conventional accounting has differentiated between costs which remain constant per unit but vary in total with production volume (variable costs) and those costs which remain constant irrespective of the total actual volume over a relevant range of production (fixed costs). Certain fixed costs are viewed by critics of conventional management accounting as actually being long-term variable costs which vary with measures of activity other than production volume and in a manner not concomitant with output. These have traditionally been apportioned on the basis of arbitrary allocation rules devoid of any apparent cause-and-effect link. Commonly used volume-based 'cost drivers' for allocating short-term variable costs include direct labour hours, machine hours and material value (all of which are volume-based). The same bases are also often used to allocate costs which have little bearing to activity volume changes and result in cost tracing, which is regarded as inaccurate.

Long-term costs which are variable with activity but not production volume are related to complexity, and increasing the volume of production does not increase the utilisation of support services such as set-ups, expediting, stock movements and scheduling activities, whereas augmenting the range of products will increase support costs rapidly. Increased product diversity may increase the documentation and record-keeping activities associated with product batches since the number of set-ups increases when production lines utilising flexible technology switch from one product to another to increase the range of production. Under a conventional costing system, these increased record-keeping costs become part of overhead and are allocated to products using an application base such as direct labour. Yet it is not direct labour utilisation or production volume which is responsible for the increased record-keeping costs but some other measure of activity which represents increased product diversity. The cost drivers underlying increased record-keeping costs should mirror transactions which increase the range of output rather than the actual volume of output.

The choice of cost drivers for activity-based costs should thus be based on factors which capture transactions, such as inspection hours, number of inspections undertaken, production lots manufactured, set-ups, shipments, orders and even the number of vendors. Figure 4.5 shows the allocation of costs such as factory, space, customer services, maintenance etc. for three products which in effect draw differently on three resources. Volume based cost allocations does not capture the complexity driven resource utilization for the three products. Figure 4.6, which uses individual cost drivers for three products, produces more acceptable allocations by accounting for the perceived usage of each cost category (see Cokins; 2002 for an extended discussion). But what constitutes an activity for costing purposes needs clarification.

Figure 4.5 Traditional Costing can be Misleading

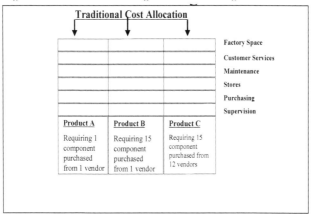

Figure 4.6 ABC Stresses Consumption

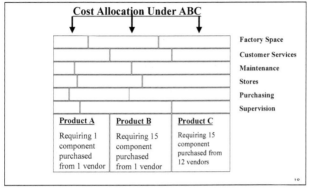

What is an Activity?

A degree of subjectivity and judgement always influences one's appreciation of activities which organizations engage in and the manner in which one activity might be conceptually extricated from a core of interrelated activities. In practice, organizations may seek to adopt a simplified prescriptive approach to developing an activity accounting system as follows: The first step in determining an activity's cost is to ascertain which factors determine the amount of resources required by the activity. The aim is to make the pattern of costs reflect the usage of resources on activities. The technology used in the activity may be seen to determine the amount of resources used in the activity and therefore the demand for the activity's output and the size of the activity's cost pool. Thus assessing an order for creditworthiness for example may involve a certain amount of staff time, data and paper processing and the use of telecommunications. It is the technical operations required which determine the resource requirement of the activity. Ideally, the attribution of costs to activities should reflect this technology by tracing costs empirically on the basis of the activity's resource driver and ultimately, resource consumption (see Figure 4.7). Often judgement, interviews, diaries and informal records are used in estimating the resource requirements of an activity.

Figure 4.7 ABC Highlights Activities

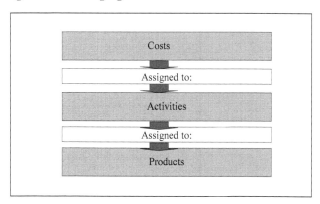

Where costs can justifiably be directly assigned on a volume basis say, machine hours, this should be the preferred option. If some other activity acts as a cost driver, then such a non-volume base is appropriate. There will typically be resources which have no recognisable driver options. These should not be assigned to individual products and services (see Figure 4.8).

Figure 4.8 Cost Assignment Options

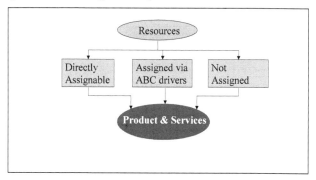

An activity should be capable of being viewed as separate from other activities and the output of the activity should be amenable to explanation, ideally by only one factor (the cost driver). This will demonstrate how costs change with variable demands for the activity's output. The driver chosen should be deduced using empirical evidence and may be specific to the firm. There are two usual types of drivers:

(1) <u>The volume or activity output</u> - Examples include the number of set-ups and the number of quality inspections.

(2) <u>Activity complexity</u> - For example, creditworthiness checks may depend not only on order size but on the type of credit arrangement required by the customer; they may be influenced by the customer or by the total size of likely demands – such as the number of products, customers and suppliers – and by the technology and the organizational structure.

The costs derived from ABC are of a different nature to costs derived from a traditional costing system. They are argued to represent the costs of activities at a time when the firm is able to rearrange its operating activities. During shorter time-periods, such factors as labour contracts or indivisible capacity (which technically cannot be reduced in the short run) may prevent any reduction in activity costs. Sometimes, the inability of rearranging operating activities relates to managerial decisions about activities, which may reside with functional managers not directly responsible for the activities under consideration. Consequently, halting production of some product seen as expensive in activity cost terms will not automatically lead to cost reductions because the underlying resource expenditure does not cease.

A numerical illustration is discussed below to show how product costs may be viewed as distorted by conventional product-costing and how activity accounting approach can provide a potential remedy. Consider the CD Company which manufactures four products P1, P2, P3 and P4. Other costs are as follows: direct labour hour (DLH) cost = £5 per hour; direct material cost (DM) = £10 per ton; variable factory overhead (VFOH) cost = £9,900; fixed factory overhead (FFOH) cost = £20,460. The FFOH costs relate to set-ups and handling. The products have different selling prices and are produced in differently sized batches as shown in Table 4.1. Suppose we use direct labour hours to allocate overhead costs, we would first calculate the overhead application rate:

Overhead application rate =
　Total OH/Total DLH
　　(£9,900 + £20,460)/((10 x 2) + (100 x 2) + (10 x 4) + (100 x 4))
　　= £46/DLH

Now we can calculate costs for P1, P2, P3 and P4
Table 4.2 shows the calculated product costs and Table 4.3 identifies the profitability of each product.

Table 4.1 Data for CD Company

Product	Selling Price (£)	Units per batch	DLH (per unit)	DM (tons per unit)
P1	350	10	2	2.5
P2	150	100	2	2.5
P3	450	10	4	5
P4	240	100	4	5

Table 4.2 Traditional Costing For CD's Products

Product	DM	DL	FOH	Product
P1	(25 x £10)	(2 x £5)	(2 x £46)	£127
P2	(25 x £10)	(2 x £5)	(2 x £46)	£127
P3	(5 x £10)	(4 x £5)	(4 x £46)	£254
P4	(5 x £10)	(4 x £5)	(4 x £46)	£254

Table 4.3 What are the Profits?

Product	Profits
P1	£223
P2	£23
P3	£196
P4	(£14)

Using activity based costing, set-ups and handlings may be used as the cost drivers for these two overhead activities. Table 4.4. provides the relevant activity data. The cost drivers may then be calculated on this basis:

DL + VFOH = £5 + (£9,900/660 DLH) = £20/DLH
Setup cost   = £8,184/8 = £1,023
Handling cost = £12,276/6 = £2,046

Table 4.4 Activity Based Costing Data for CD

Product	No. of Set-Ups per Batch *	No. of Handlings per Batch **
P1	1	1
P2	3	2
P3	1	1
P4	3	2

* Total setup costs = £8,184   ** Total handling costs = £12,276

Table 4.5 ABC Costings for CD

Product	DM	DL + VOH	Setups	Handling	Product Cost
P1	(2.5 x £10)	(2 x £20)	(£1023/10)	(£2046/10)	£375
P2	(2.5 x £10)	(2 x £20)	(3 x £1023/100)	(2x£2046/100)	£137
P3	(5 x £10)	(4 x £20)	(£1023/10)	(£2046/10)	£440
P4	(5 x £10)	(4 x £20)	(3 x £1023/100)	(2x£2046/100)	£202

P1	(£15)
P2	£13
P3	£10
P4	£38

Note that the profitability rankings are altered. Under traditional costing the order of profitability for the four products is: P1, P3, P2, P4. Under ABC: P4, P2, P3, P1.

An ABC system can potentially help companies avoid dropping products erroneously because of misleading product costs. This example shows that traditional costing systems can report lower profits for larger-volume products that consume more of the cost driver. These products will likely be the first to be deleted where product deletion decisions are made based on individual product profitability. Subsequently, the low profits for the remaining smaller-volume products which consume more of the cost driver will also cause their elimination from product offerings. Incorrect product discontinuance decisions can lead to more product discontinuance and/or outsourcing. Ultimately, very few products are left which imperils the viability of the enterprise (the "death spiral").

When to Replace a Costing System

The idea that an understanding of activities is necessary to manage costs is intuitive. Recognising problems with costing systems is also in part intuitive. A number of signals can emerge which suggest the need to modernise a company's costing system:

Functional managers want to drop seemingly profitable products; profit margins are difficult to explain; hard to make products show big profits; functional departments have their own costing systems; the accounting department spends a lot of time on special projects; the company maintains a high-margin niche; competitors' prices are unrealistically low; customers do not mind price increases; the results of bids are not readily understood; vendor bids are lower than expected; reported costs change because of new financial accounting regulations.

A cost system need not measure absolutely everything down to the finest degree (Cooper, 1989). Taking infinitesimal measurements of each portion of material input and each minute of direct labour expanded can be expensive and time-consuming. The expense may be deemed necessary only when the consequences of relying on otherwise inaccurate information are severe. For instance, when profit margins are miniscule and the market is rapidly changing and uncertain, basing decisions on cost data which is considered to lack accuracy can put a company at a disadvantage very rapidly. Under such circumstances, cost accuracy may be important. But often it may not be worthwhile for the enterprise to expand extensive resources to obtain such figures. Figure 4.9 identifies the growth of costs alongside the rising level of cost understanding derived from accounting systems. Clearly, the level of cost detail sought is an important consideration in implementing activity accounting. Deciding upon the level of strategic versus operational detail sought of the accounting system is also relevant. Information for macro-level decisions would require less information collection than that intended for micro-operational use.

A cost system which trades off the cost of measurement and the cost of errors from inaccurate information in a way that minimises total cost may be regarded as desirable (see Figure 4.10).

Figure 4.9 The Cost of Understanding Costs

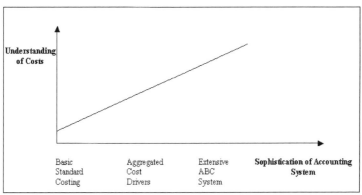

Economists would suggest that the optimal system exists at the point where the marginal cost of improving the system's accuracy exactly equals the marginal benefit.. Competitive conditions are dynamic, so the cost of errors changes. Similarly, as information-processing technology changes, so does the cost of measurement. An optimal cost system is essentially a moving target.

It is important to remember that with product diversity increases – as high volume is mixed with low volume, or as labour intensity is coupled with automation – costs are more likely to be skewed. To achieve a desired level of accuracy, enterprises may have to spend more on measurements than when products are more homogeneous. If they do not, their cost systems will be seen as inadequate if not obsolete.

Figure 4.10 Cost of Accuracy versus the Cost of Errors

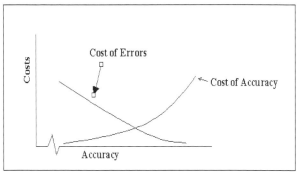

System Design Issues

Activity accounting may be viewed as extending the variable costing rationale in an attempt to render cost determinations more useful for managerial purposes. Whereas variable costing focuses on short-term volume-related costs, an activity accounting cost determination includes long-term variable costs, which traditionally are grounded in overhead cost pools. Accounting nevertheless goes beyond a contribution margin analysis in that it addresses cost behaviour quantitatively in terms of both short-run volume changes and longer-term cost trends that are independent of scale changes. This approach offers an element of rationality and compelling logic which managers often readily identify with (Bhimani and Bromwich, 2001). However, the new forms of economic representations which activity accounting engenders may not be easily absorbed and deployed within organizations. Established practices relating to the release of information as well as its distribution and use need to be heeded in the implementation of any new information system including activity based costing. Organizational factors should be regarded as of equal significance as technical logic.

The search for appropriate cost drivers forces managers and accountants to reconsider operational processes in a comprehensive manner and within an economic and strategic management frame of reference. The identification of value-added and non-value-added activities required for the implementation of an activity accounting system is important. Such accounting information can help identify more desirable production strategies, such as the design of products with common parts, the discontinuance of low volume products necessitating complex manufacturing processes, and the identification of cost drivers which can lead to the adoption of altered production technologies. Activity accounting can offer an enterprise information not only about the profitability of its output, but also about the gains that may emanate from altering organizational processes. In budgeting, activity-based budgets can usefully point to significant planning and control dimensions. Budgets can appear as matrices for different departments, whereby activities are represented in columns and required or expected resources are placed in rows. Naturally, the representation of activity accounting information needs to be formatted and structured to fit the organizational context and its idiosyncratic deployment of financial and operational information.

It has been said that one benefit of ABC is that it provides non-financial managers with data that is potentially more useful than traditional product-costing information. By linking overheads to activities rather than products or periods, ABC provides the benefit of making cost absorption more transparent. This enables non-financial managers to carry out inter-unit cost comparisons. Improvements between plants can thus be made and subsequent inter-temporal comparisons of costs can be effected. But such comparisons implicate issues of organizational culture and raises important considerations concerning the ethos of the enterprise and whether this aligns with the information sharing and motivational premises embedded in the activity accounting system.

Cooper (1996) notes that an ABC system can support a company's transition to a "lean enterprise" which he sees as characterised by:

Adoption Of Just-In-Time (Jit) Production.
Total Quality Management (Tqm).
Team-Based Work Arrangements.
Supportive Supplier Relations.
Improved Customer Satisfaction.

He believes that for ABC in fact to hinder the spread of the 'lean enterprise', the information it generates must be sufficiently contrary to the basis of the lean enterprise that it forces managers to readopt mass-production practices (i.e., batch size greater than 1 and defects effectively greater than 0) rather than lean-enterprise practices (i.e., batch size approaching 1 and defects approaching 0). In this sense, ABC supports the shift to TQM and JIT. Since both ABC and the "lean enterprise" lead to reduced defect levels, there is no obvious conflict between the two levels. ABC systems report much higher costs of defects than traditional cost systems. This helps managers begin to pursue a policy of zero defects.

Clearly, the activity accounting perspective has relevant ties with quality management, just-in-time systems and the adoption of flexible organizational technologies. Over the past few years, activity accounting techniques have been documented to have other widespread implications. Links exist between the ABC and throughput accounting, business process reengineering, economic value added, transfer pricing, life cycle costing, zero based budgeting, functional analysis, benchmarking, capital budgeting and target costing among others (Bhimani et al., 2012). Activity accounting systems need to achieve a balance with the particular ways in which these other managerial philosophies work at the enterprise level. Perhaps for this reason, there are about as many distinct activity accounting systems in operation today as there are companies deploying them.

Although many companies prefer activity-based costing to traditional cost accounting systems for measuring resource consumption, some companies have experienced problems with ABC. Some studies indicate one important reason for unsuccessful implementations of ABC is that companies have overemphasised architectural and software design issues of ABC systems and failed to pay sufficient attention to organizational issues such as the presence of top management support and training. Survey study results indicate also that level of linkage of ABC to competitive strategy is an important determinant of the success of an ABC implementation. ABC should be linked to a firm's competitive strategy regarding organizational design, new product development, product mix and pricing and technology.

Training in the logic and operation of ABC is also important because it helps people understand how ABC differs from traditional cost accounting and how ABC might be viewed as a possibly superior economic measurement and information system. If individuals do not understand why or how ABC works, they are likely to disregard or misunderstand it. Moreover, a broad cross-section of employees should be involved in decisions about the initial decisions to invest in ABC, the design and implementation of ABC systems, and the use of ABC information for analysis and action.

When ABC is owned only by finance executives, there is the danger that it might be used only to satisfy their needs, which often relate to status within the accounting profession and the departmental culture, rather than the concerns of operational managers. Some companies have not had good implementation experiences because accountants have retained ownership or have not succeeded in sharing ownership with non-accountants. The consequence can be a repeating cycle of ABC designs without corresponding management action. Clear system design considerations must encompass organizational rather than just technical accounting concerns.

Economic Logic and Organizational Realities

At times, economic logic is pursued too fervently at the cost of enhanced organizational functioning. When simplistic and overly focused views of accounting systems take precedence over fundamental aspects of organizational action, unfortunate consequences often follow. At times traditional economic models assume that a company engages in production to meet market requirements so as to enhance profits. Individuals, however, do not operate on the basis of conceptual economic models. Their behaviour at individual and group levels often exhibit "erring" which cannot be readily subsumed in economic conceptualisations of enterprise processes.

Little recognition is given to the processing of information, executive idiosyncrasies, internal dynamics and the play of social interaction in classical economics. Since many 'rational' management tools such as ABC systems closely adhere to the classical economic perspective, problems of implementation at the organizational level ensue.

Executives live by behavioural rules of thumb, sometimes of their own making, to deal with complex and risky situations. A situation's complexity and uncertainty will dictate reliance on such rules. Indeed, idiosyncrasies can become embedded in the structure of an organization. They can ossify within the enterprise's systems of operations. Attempts to implement logics of operation or decision-making which have external roots will encounter resistance in the face of such institutionalised idiosyncrasies.

Another problem which can confront the implementation of a novel cost management approach relates to shifts in the logic of production. For example, the management of vast amounts of information concerning specific functional activities can lead to organizations to invest in information systems which prioritise such information. When the dynamics of operating processes alter so as to bring about greater interdependence and integration of organizational activities, older 'legacy' systems are ill-prepared to face the altered environment.

Some enterprises facing greater complexity and interdependency adopt accounting in an attempt to deal with their interdependent processes. Organizations with the greatest level of cross-functional activities may be ones that can benefit most from ABC. Nevertheless, many such companies have retained their traditional organizational forms and procedures. Highly developed traditional structures – which may have been cost efficient in the past – can raise important barriers to the implementation of cross-functional change. Consequently, ABC may be more difficult to implement in these enterprises than might be assumed. Naturally, just as with the implementation of any financial management or costing approach, the organizational context must be assessed to establish alignment and acceptance of the application.

When top management is not fully supportive of an ABM effort, the exercise is likely to falter. Naturally if there is no 'buy-in' or ownership, then managers will not give the initiative time, nor any other scarce resource. If it is accepted that cost management systems serve financial, operational and strategic purposes then it must be recognised that an activity accounting system need widespread support from the outset. It is important to understand how information from a new cost system is likely to be used. This in turn can guide project design issues. Projects should not be viewed as a "finance" project. It may be preferable to place a marketing, operations or engineering person at the head of the initiative. Consequently, ABM will be perceived as a management tool to serve management decision making.

Additionally, it is important to involve other staff members with the identification of activities and cost drivers to be undertaken primarily by non-accountants. This is so that those most knowledgeable about the work identify what drives processes. It is at times the case that when non-accountants are involved in creating an activity accounting system, they can be more likely to use the information it generates. It is also the case that where consultants are used they may want to impose the same answers that they have used in previous engagements rather than find answers that are company specific. It is important that an activity accounting system reflect the 'worldview' of management and the culture of the organization to the extent possible. Extra organizational solutions may not fit in with an enterprise's specific culture.

Sometimes, activity accounting systems reflect the predilection of operating and financial personnel who seek the ability to view cost in multiple dimensions and minute detail. Project teams may want ABC to include product costing with detailed activity levels, customer costing and distribution channel costing. They may want activity accounting to include process costing, value-added analysis and cost of quality. Information may also relate to variable, semi-variable and fixed cost differentiations and there will be categorisation in terms of unit-level, batch-level, product-level, process-sustaining, facility-sustaining, customer-sustaining and decision-levels of costs. Such requirements can be costly and over-detailed. It is essential to match the complexity of activity accounting information to its relative ease of digestibility by its users and the explicit requirements of managers desiring activity accounting information. Whilst too much information may be problematic, so may too little detail. Thus, investigating users' needs and the activity accounting system's intended role is important to establish at the outset.

Some activity accounting projects are hindered by problems relating to activity data collection. There may be problems in terms of definitions of individual activities; the level of reliability that the activity data has; and the methods of collecting the activity information. In terms of data reliability, it is important to note that data gathering may suffer from intentional bias. When a member of staff is questioned about how their time is spent, it is important to ensure that the most recent time frame does not reflect 'seasonality of activities'. Also, some individuals may fear the loss of their jobs, while others may bias data to make favourite products, activities or functions look like they are performing better than they actually are. Idle time or non-value-added tasks can be masked. The issue of data collection is important. When selecting activity bases and cost drivers, some companies may give preference to drivers that are already being gathered or drivers that will be easier to collect. Naturally, ease of collection should tally with the value ascribed to the information sought. The structure of the enterprise itself will shape information flows and data collected. It is useful to recognize that activity accounting systems may deliberately sidestep the functional structure of organizations in making assignments to activities and then to products or customers. While they may yield valuable information about activities, these systems may not focus on departmental information as a matter of intent.

Behavioural issues may govern what is collected and what not and how data collection is perceived. Ignoring the views of system users and employees can endanger the success of an activity accounting system since departmental groups may view this as a threat. They may fear loss of power, prestige and importance in the company. Some managers may consider that activity information will be used to decrease the size of their departments or lead to outsourcing of the entire department. Consequently, department heads who perceive a potential loss of power or resources may try to subvert the activity accounting system. Activity based analyses may provide new and different views of an organization and its performance. Acting on these new views may require a cultural departure from tradition. Thus the prevalence of activity accounting techniques in practice reflects not just belief that such systems are logical in financial terms. Organizational complexities, cultural preferences and institutional forces influence activity accounting adoption decisions too.

5

MEASURES THAT PERFORM

Different companies use different approaches to measuring and rewarding performance. Jeff Bezos, Founder and CEO of Amazon.com says: 'We pay very low cash compensation relative to most companies. We have no incentive compensation of any kind. And the reason we don't is because it is detrimental to teamwork' (Fortune 3/12/2012, p.36). This is true of most employees though Amazon does pay senior officers some restricted stock that becomes valuable over time. Netflix has no vacation policy; employees take time off as they need as long as they get the job done. There are no strict compensation rules – workers choose their stock-to-cash ratio. There are no formal titles. Netflix's Head of Human Resources says: 'If you're looking for perks, this is the wrong place' (Fortune 6/12/2010, p. 52). Voser, CEO of Royal Dutch Shell believes that 'Everyone needs to know what is expected of them. You need to measure performance. In a race like this, you don't get gold medals for personal bests, you get them for winning and I will be setting top-down targets to get Shell fitter and performing' (Fortune, 20/7/2009). Every enterprise will tend to set up its own specific reward system and determine how performance measurement will operate within it.

The Goals of Performance Measures

Performance evaluation is considered an important aspect of financial management systems. Effective performance evaluation is complex and difficult to achieve. Many management commentators believe that performance measures should be quantifiable and should encompass all aspects of performance that relate to outcomes. But these requirements are often in conflict because many relevant aspects of performance are intangible and difficult to quantify. Some aims of performance measures are:
- encourage goal congruence (i.e., the alignment of employees' goals with those of the company as a whole);

- focus on future operating results;
- include both financial and non-financial criteria;
- provide a means of communication between operations and finance functions.

One criticism of traditional performance evaluation systems is that their focus is mainly on financial information. Criteria based on sales, earnings, return on investment, and budget variances have dominated performance standards traditionally. While these measures help managers evaluate financial performance, they do not lend themselves to the measurement of management effectiveness, operational productivity, product quality, and asset utilisation. They also tend to report historical performance (i.e., what has happened) rather than predict future performance (i.e., what will happen).

Performance measures that concentrate on budget and production variances do not necessarily indicate whether an operation is performing effectively relative to the goals of the organization. The incorporation of such traditional measures into evaluation programmes can cause employees to behave in ways that are opposed to the overall goals of the company. For example, if a single performance measure (e.g., a standard cost variance) is overemphasised in an employee's performance evaluation, the employee is encouraged to make decisions that maximise his or her personal performance in terms of that single measure. But such an isolated focus may not necessarily be compatible with maximising corporate welfare. When management control systems stress performance measures and achievement targets that fail to emphasise the articulated goals and objectives of the organization as a whole, a departmentally focused or even a highly individualistic outlook may be promoted by the system and pursued by managers. Jack Welch former head of GE ("Stop the BS budgets," *Fortune*, 26/6/06) believes that: 'The budgeting process as it currently stands at most companies does exactly what you'd never want. It hides growth opportunities. It promotes bad behavior – especially when market conditions change midstream and people still try to "make the number". It has an uncanny way of sucking the energy and fun out of an organization'. Why? Because most budgeting is disconnected from reality. The goal of the people in the field is: Come up with targets that they absolutely positively think they can hit. Targets are directly linked to their remuneration. They construct plans with layer upon layer of conservative thinking. Meanwhile, back at headquarters, executives are also preparing for the budget review, but with exactly the opposite agenda. Welch says that when both sides are alone, they will crow among themselves about how they managed to get the other side to exactly reach the targets they wanted.

Efforts to improve traditional evaluation systems have emphasised the need to evaluate the ability of employees to increase the long-run effectiveness of their business units in harmony with organizational goals. Therefore, effectively articulating organizational goals, strategies for achieving the goals, and performance measures are all relevant to a performance evaluation system. The identification of goals, strategies and measures is always a complex exercise and a deep understanding of organizational issues is critical to this process.

Designing Effective Performance Measurement Systems

Performance goals should be clearly defined and stated in terms of specific outcomes that are measurable. Performance measures can then be linked to these outcomes. The participation of employees in developing goals and in defining performance measures influences their drive to achieve these goals. The realisation of goals is affected by how far employees:

- **view the goals as necessary and attainable;**
- **have control over the outcomes that affect performance evaluation.**

In other words, belief in what is being pursued and the perception of controllability are important to achieving targets. Much research has been undertaken on organizational participants' amenability to enhancing their productive performance. In a review of performance and participative budgeting investigations the finding was reported that "performance is the most frequently reported and statistically significantly dependent variable associated with participation" (Chalos and Poon, 2001, p.173). A system aimed at evaluating performance may thus begin with the determination of goals and the participation of individuals affected by the pursuit of these goals and their attainment. Strategies may have to be developed to achieve the goals and the expected outcomes specified. Performance measures which are consistent with the desired outcomes need to be established and systems have to be developed to collect and evaluate performance measures. The effectiveness of a performance evaluation system depends on whether the organization's goals are understood, pursued, and ultimately achieved, bearing in mind that employee participation in goal setting is key to enhancing performance. This can be represented as follows:

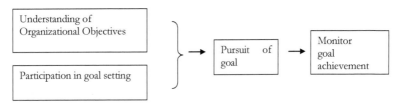

An area of important research in accounting is <u>agency theory</u> which has stressed the motivational aspects of incentives in aligning principal-agent pursuits. This body of research has, however, not extensively concerned itself with managers' participation in designing their incentive systems. Lack of such participation can lead to problems. Consider, for instance, "forced ranking" systems whereby employees are ranked against one another and grades are distributed along a bell curve. Companies such as Hewlett-Packard, Ford, Microsoft and Cisco have implemented such systems. This may be because they "facilitate budgeting and guard against spineless managers who are too afraid to jettison poor performers" (Boyle, 2001, p.103) according to proponents of forced rankings. At Ford, five percent of employees who get the lowest grade C are not eligible for a bonus that year. Two C's in a row are grounds for dismissal. Jack Welch, ex-CEO of GE, believes that: "Not removing that bottom ten percent … is not only a management failure but false kindness as well" (cited in Boyle, 2001, p.104). This view is not shared across all employees in organizations using forced ranking. Many employees consider forced distributions as discriminatory grading and have taken legal action against their employers. The performance measurement system opted for by the organizations needs to align with employee pursuits with employee input into measurement systems design being present.

Aligning corporate with departmental and individual goals is important. But monitoring changing organizational goals and linkages with individual performance mechanisms is also a concern. A number of surveys reveal that companies expect to keep changing their performance measurement systems in the future. This is true of enterprises operating in many different industries. Organizations which are moving away from repetitive manufacturing toward more complex production environments where qualitative criteria, team effort, communication skills and intellectual agility are key issues, tend also to engage in very careful and continuous redesign of their performance measurement systems.

A performance measurement system may require change for different reasons:
- decrease in profitability
- change in strategy
- search for enhanced shareholder value
- redesign of business processes
- new technology
- new competition
- attempts to attract or retain employees

Recognition by an organization that an altered performance measurement system is required is tied to its search for ways to grow and add to shareholder value (Maisel, 2001). The following factors are considered to be key to a successful performance measurement system.

- it must be integrated with the overall strategy of the business
- there must be a system of feedback and review
- the performance measurement system must be comprehensive
- the system must be supported throughout the organization
- measures need to be fair and achievable
- the system needs to be simple, clear and understandable

But the viability of a performance measurement system change is influenced by organizational culture. Many companies prefer to continue employing traditional accounting measures rather than use novel approaches to performance measurement because the culture of the organization is not conducive to the introduction of new measures. Organizational culture can be a significant determinant of the success of an information system. Research indicates that in some contexts, aligning the ethos of a management accounting system to the organizational culture orientation of employees using the system positively influences their perception of the system's success. Conversely, when organizational culture is at odds with the basis of the performance information system, resistance can result.

Why New Performance Measures?

Over the past century, a shift in industrial activities has been witnessed across many nations away from manufacturing and towards service-based sectors. Many commentators on management practices and financial methodologies have suggested that performance measurement systems have not kept pace with this shift. The stress has remained on mechanical and scientific conceptions of industrial activities which have tended to underscore financial and other quantitative measures. The focus has remained on maximizing the utilisation of the factors of production through measures of efficiency, stakeholders' return on capital and on the management of tangible assets. The adoption of flexible organizational technologies during the last decades of the twentieth century brought into relief the desirability for systems designs which seek to capture the requirements of operating decisions such as those entailed in process improvement, and product design, as well as strategic ones such as product mix, customer profitability and sourcing issues.

Beyond this, the advent of internet technologies and the growing perception that intangibles such as brands, intellectual capital, patent rights and organizational agility need to be assessed, tracked and leveraged, have fuelled the search for relevant and legitimate performance measurement systems salient. Kaplan and Norton (1996, p.8) perceive the need to identify the value of a company's intellectual and other intangible assets, but warn that the "difficulties in placing a reliable financial value on such assets as process capabilities, employee skills, motivation, customer loyalty ... will likely preclude them from ever being recognised in organizational balance sheets". Other management thinkers are less sceptical of the potential which restructured performance measurement systems offer for contributing to managerial decision-making in altering organizational environments. Supplementing financial with non-financial measures is increasingly seen as appropriate in the design of performance measures.

Although traditional accounting measures are dominant in practice, there is evidence that new measures of performance especially value-based metrics are gaining popularity. Many firms use the balance scorecard approach as well as other performance systems. Whilst the balance scorecard addresses financial and non-financial aspects of performance, value-based metrics are more focused on financial performance and shareholders. Value-based metrics seek to combine three characteristics of enterprises - cash flow generated, capital invested to generate the cash flows and the cost of capital of the investment. Amongst performance measures introduced by the organizations included in the study over the previous three years, the balanced scorecard seemed most popular (see Figure 5.1).

An organization's ability to operate successfully depends to a large extent on the availability of information upon which its managers can act. The role of information about performance, whether for use within the enterprise or for external parties, is often regarded as crucial in determining economic or commercial viability. The pace of change of business activities and the need to remain responsive to market pressures means that a performance measurement system cannot remain static. Changes in production methods and in the organization of work have led academics, consultants and commentators on industrial practices to encourage rethinking of performance evaluation approaches. In the case of manufacturing companies, critics of traditional performance measurement systems have pointed to the existence of a drift between fundamental changes in the way in which manufacturing processes now take place and the traditional performance measures being used in many companies. Work organization methods such as just-in-time purchasing and production have transformed production methods even in relatively small companies. Consequently, it is claimed that similarly radical alterations need to be made to the ways in which other enterprise activities are monitored.

In Search of Balance

The issue of appropriate performance measures is highly significant because it can affect commercial success. In the present economic climate, many companies are looking for appropriate information about their internal processes to establish ways of cost cutting, of enhancing performance and generally, of building better products in shrinking markets. Many companies are finding that the need for accurate and comprehensive information about their activities is increasingly intense.
The results of many surveys suggest that financial based measures exhibit widespread deployment. Metrics which track adherence to budgets, financial yield and achievement of desired profits and cash flow criteria are prevalent. Nevertheless, it is also evident that organizations show interest in measures which help align operational activities with strategic pursuits.

Kaplan and Norton (2001) also stress the value of non- financial measures and link all relevant performance measures to 'strategy and vision'. They combine financial measures of performance with operational-level measures of performance (e.g., innovativeness and customer satisfaction). They advocate that employees at all levels should be given the flexibility to achieve their respective objectives and suggest that clearly defined goals should be established before being implemented through a 'scorecard' (see below). Non-financial performance measures (e.g., concerning product and/or service quality, and timing) are part of a larger, firm-wide strategic plan. Thus, both firm-specific financial and non-financial performance goals should be defined, measured and integrated to some degree. However, financial performance measures are to be used primarily to the extent that they aid the firm in attaining its strategic goals.

The need to support the organization's strategic mission through performance measures is felt clearly by many companies. Table 5.1 identifies commonly used financial and non-financial measures which can be altered to address more directly the processes and/or functional structure specific to an enterprise.

To link strategic objectives and business performance, an understanding must be developed about what an organization's strategy is and about the form of information which reflects and supports such strategy. Information which attempts to provide top management with a balanced view of the overall performance of the business might include information from a number of different perspectives. The following might feature significantly:

Figure 5.1 Performance measures recently introduced or being considered for introduction

```
Balanced        Scorecard
approach

Economic  value   added
(EVA®)

Value drivers

Shareholder value analysis
(SVA)

Economic profit

Cash  flow  return  on
investment (CFROI)

Target cash flow

Return on capital employed
(ROCE)

Target profit
```

(1) *Customers:* many organizations consider that understanding what their customers think of their performance is an important way of ensuring that performance in key areas is up to the desired standard. It is generally the case that protecting and developing an existing customer base is much more cost effective than constantly finding new customers. This is so for on and off-line business activities. However, measures that indicate the company's performance in this respect often do not form part of a company's regular reporting.

(2) *External environment:* the need to monitor and understand the dynamics of the business and competitive environment is seen as important. Many companies do not formally decide what should be

monitored, how and how often and on assigning responsibility for both collection and interpretation.

(3) *Processes and activities:* by understanding processes and their constituent activities, organizations can highlight areas of concern and focus attention and action accordingly. One possible advantage of activity-based approaches to managers is the insight provided into the key processes by which a company's strategy is realised. All too often, reporting remains functionally-based, whereby managers learn little about key processes that cut across functional boundaries.

(4) *continuous improvement:* **how well an organization and its people are learning and developing can be crucial to the firm's long-term competitiveness. Some companies have in place formal procedures for measuring and tracking the skills and effectiveness of their people.**

(5)*Financial:* **this will continue to be an important measure of overall success.**

Table 5.1 Financial and non-financial measures commonly used in assessing performance

WORKING CAPITAL	GENERAL PRODUCTION	DEMAND
Cashflow	Capital utilisation	Market share
Creditor days	Inventory	Orders on hand
Debtor days		
CAPITAL MARKET	PROCESS	PRODUCT
Asset value per share	Manufacturing lead time	Price
Dividend cover	per cent rework and reject	Product quality
Dividend per share	per cent yield on production	
Earnings per share	Schedule adherence	
Price/earnings ratio	Set-up time	
(FINANCIAL) RETURN	LABOUR	CUSTOMER
Capital turnover	Direct labour productivity	Complaints
Working capital turnover	Indirect labour productivity	Warranty claims
Profit to turnover	Employee turnover	Repeat orders
Return on capital employed		On-time delivery
Profit		
Total shareholder returns		
Profit per employee		
Economic value added		
Sales per employee		
LENDER SECURITY	SUPPLIERS	INNOVATIVENESS
Gearing	Number of suppliers	New product frequency
Interest cover	Supplier lead time	New product time to market

The appropriate balance of the different perspectives will vary across organizations so a process for identifying individual requirements is essential. Management information may need to reflect the processes and activities of the company perhaps as it reflects the organizational structure. The consequences for roles and responsibilities within the organization will have to be evaluated critically. At times, management information that is inadequate, will underpin existing organization structures. Challenging and changing performance measures and making individual managers' responsibilities and accountabilities visible can be unsettling to managers. Outdated or irrelevant measures can thereby remain attractive to an individual manager if they show that he or she is performing well.
What is also important is to consider how the culture of the organization ties in with the design elements of performance measurement systems and reward structures. Organization culture can be thought of as beliefs and expectations shared by members of an organization. These beliefs and expectations produce rules for behaviour – norms – that powerfully shape the comportment of individuals and groups in the organization. Both performance measurement systems and reward systems can be regarded as shaping organizational culture. The manner in which performance is measured – the elements which are emphasised and those discounted – has a direct bearing on the expectations placed on the workforce.

Consider, for instance, the rise of "work teams" as an organizational structure favoured by many enterprises. Creating team-based organizational structures supports a number of business practices that have increased, including business process re-engineering, team production, total quality management and the creation of more decentralised organizational structures. Yet there is little evidence which links teaming and performance outcomes or that enterprises which alter their structures directly align the change with their performance systems.
The evidence on corporate changes in performance measurement systems suggests that no optimal set of measures has emerged in practice or theory to monitor comprehensively enterprise performance. Performance measures should be contextually determined. Certainly, a general roadmap approach may suggest a focus on some aspect of quality, delivery, process times and flexibility alongside the traditional working capital, accounting return and capital market financial monitors. However, a changing business climate and altered production and operational technologies and methodologies mean that performance measures useful at one time may become redundant at another. Thus a fine balance must be reached not

just between reliance on financial and non-financial performance measures but also between the characteristics and activities which underpin an enterprise's structure and culture and the choice of representative performance monitors.

As indicated above, organizations may be regarded as organisms rather than mechanisms. Understanding the organization's culture is seen as important as assessing its formal systems of control. Since the middle of the twentieth century, many French companies developed <u>Tableau de Bords</u> as performance systems which can be formal but highly customised to the managers. Tableau de Bords are developed by managers or senior operational personnel to guide their sub-unit's activities via a series of metrics. They include strategic and operational monitors rather than just financial metrics. Their structuring was organization and unit specific rather than generic.

The balanced scorecard has been presented as a more comprehensive approach to performance concerns which, like the Tableau de Bord, seeks to provide information exceeding that of financial control scorekeeping reports. By identifying the beliefs that appear to underlie culture and by making those beliefs explicit, an enterprise can assess what might contribute to its success. Financial managers and accountants who are aware of corporate and departmental cultures need flexibility of approach to cost system design. Achieving this entails communication, education, involvement, negotiation, agreement and continuous interaction with operational managers and staff.

The Balanced Scorecard

The <u>balanced scorecard</u> is an approach to performance control which must be considered in the light of an organization's broader performance system structure. Simons (2000) notes that the balanced scorecard is a complement, not a replacement, for an organization's other performance measurement and control systems. He sees performance measurement and control systems as essential tools used by effective managers in attempts to achieve their desired profit goals and strategies. These systems comprise profit planning and a variety of performance-management techniques and allow managers to balance the tensions between: profit, growth, and control; short-term versus long-term performance; expectations of different constituencies; opportunities and attention; and the differing motives of human behaviour. Properly applied, performance measurement and control systems can be used to overcome the organizational blocks that impede the potential of individuals working in modern organizations. The balanced scorecard may be considered to cast a wide net over organizational performance issues in that it is concerned with wide groups of stakeholders rather than purely shareholders.

Kaplan and Norton (2001) argue that managers focusing on a single financial measure often tend to manage for the short term, which may lead to a failure to invest in assets essential to long-term growth. Investments to obtain motivated and skilled employees and to ensure customer satisfaction often pay off only over the long term. Therefore, managers need a performance measurement system that provides balance between outcome measures (the results of past efforts) and the measures that are to drive future performance. The balanced scorecard provides such a set of measures. It is based on the premise that organizational performance needs to be viewed from four perspectives

(1) The financial perspective.
(2) The customer perspective.
(3) The internal-business-process perspective.
(4) The learning-and-growth perspective.

The framework is illustrated in Figure 5.2. The four dimensions are discussed below.

The financial perspective :

Kaplan and Norton (2001) argue that the goals of any profit seeking company are ultimately financial. Financial objectives establish the objectives and measures in the other three perspectives. It is unlikely that one financial metric can be appropriate across a wide range of business units. Financial objectives also differ at each stage of a business's life cycle. For instance, businesses in the growth stage may operate with negative cash flows and low returns on invested capital. For mature businesses, however, the overall financial objectives would probably be operating cash flow (before depreciation) and reductions in working capital.

Several financial themes drive business strategy across all stages of a business's life cycle. Measures of financial return include:

- return on investment
- return on capital employed
- return on assets

Another dimension is revenue growth and mix. Companies can assess their progress in this area by tracking the following:
- The percentage revenues from new products, services, and customers.
- Profitability of particular customers and product lines.
- Percentage of unprofitable customers.

Figure 5.2 The Balanced Scorecard Dimensions

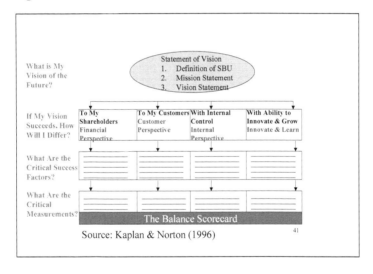

Source: Kaplan & Norton (1996)

The customer perspective

Here companies determine the customer and market segments in which they compete. As part of the customer perspective, companies identify and measure ways in which they deliver value to targeted customers and market segments. Once a business has identified and targeted its market segments, it can address the objectives and measures for these. The importance of customer satisfaction is always key. Some measures include:
- Market share;
- Customer satisfaction survey data; and
- Marketing expenses to sales ratio.

Research indicates that only when customers are completely satisfied can a company begin to pursue their buying loyalty.

The internal-business-process perspective:

For the internal-business-process perspective, managers identify the processes that are most critical for achieving customer and shareholder objectives. Managers define a complete internal-process value chain. This value chain starts with the innovation process - identifying current and future customers' needs and developing new solutions for these needs. The operations process entails delivering existing products and services to existing customers and ends with post-sales service - offering services after sale that add to the value customers receive from a company's products.

There can be specific measures for the three phases of the value chain. For example, measures for the innovation process could include the following:
- Percentage of sales from new products;
- New product introduction versus competitors';
- Times to replenish stock; and
- Production defects.

The learning-and-growth perspective:

The learning-and-growth perspective develops objectives and measures to drive organizational learning and growth. The concern here is to enable a basis for continuous organizational development and ongoing learning. Objectives in the learning-and-growth perspective provide the basis for performing on the other three perspectives. The following are three principal categories for this perspective:
- Employees' capabilities;
- Information-system capabilities; and
- Motivation, empowerment, and personal versus corporate goal alignment.

Employee capabilities are especially important, since organizations must hire individuals capable of creative problem solving and continuous improvement. Employee capabilities can be assessed through data on employee satisfaction, retention, and productivity. Possible measures include:
- Output per employee;
- Employee retention indices; and
- Training time per employee.

The Balanced Scorecard and Strategy

Managers can use the balanced scorecard as a way of expressing the firm's strategy, communicate its details, motivate people to execute plans, and enable executives to monitor results. The prime advantage is that a broad array of indicators can improve the decision making that contributes to strategic success, whether in big organizations or small, profit-focused or non-profit ones, whether at the executive level or the team level. Non-financial measures enable managers to consider more factors critical to long-term performance. These factors, flowing directly from the organization's strategy, vary from how well the organization understands its customers to how fast it innovates.

It may be that a reason managers strive for more non-financial measures is that traditional financial measures give a historical view of performance –

'through the rear-view mirror' (CMA Canada, 1999). The 'lagging' financial figures, like sales volume, help the firm keep track of the past. They often do not provide as much insight as forecasted data on quality and shipping performance for instance. In other words, financial measures tend not to offer the predictive information that are part of many non-financial metrics.

By incorporating new measures in a balanced scorecard, an organization's managers can be prepared for future competition imposed by the market it operates in, such as:

To improve performance continuously;
To implement more complex strategies;
To better run lean, decentralised organizations;
To feed systems for organizational learning; and
To drive organizational change.

CMA Canada (1999) has noted that while managers have found they need a broader set of measures to manage within the organization, they are also perceiving the need for a broader set of measures to identify external issues and manage external relationships. The organization's success may depend on managing the partners, suppliers, customers, shareholders, and other stakeholders via which the organization creates value. To this end, a balanced scorecard can help in a variety of ways:

To sense the demands of markets, competition, and society.
To broaden and deepen supply-chain relationships.
To broaden and deepen relationships with stakeholders.
To demonstrate accountability for performance.

Ass organizations develop balanced scorecards, they can apply them in at least three ways: as part of a performance improvement system, as part of a strategic management system, and as part of an internal and external accountability system. Using the balanced scorecard as a performance improvement system allows managers to deliver better results with current plans and processes. Top executives who are largely satisfied with strategic execution, can use a balanced set of measures to drive continuous improvement such as with a total quality management initiative. They can rely on the powerful linking of measures, in a cascading fashion, to the drivers of performance at every level. This cascading enables firm-wide, not just factory-wide, improvement of performance.

Kaplan and Norton (2001) believe that executives can translate the corporate vision, communicate strategy down through the organization, integrate business and financial plans to deliver the strategy, and stimulate feedback that indicates how to change the strategy to increase its effectiveness. Each of these processes is useful by themselves. But together they can play a decisive role in organizational success, especially when a firm launches a new strategy or undergoes considerable change.

Another way to apply the balanced scorecard is as part of a corporate accountability system. When managers use measures as a performance-improvement system, or as a strategic management system, they are largely restricting themselves to an internal focus. They consequently develop strong internal accountability – systems for defining goals, meeting them, and gathering intelligence. Such a focus is seen to be appropriate not just for profit seeking but also for not-for-profit organizations.

The Effective Implementation of a Balanced Scorecard

A number of key elements affect the success of a balanced scorecard solution. One must naturally be that it is deployable. The balanced scorecard methodology is only valuable when rolled out across all divisions and down all management levels. If only the management team knows what the strategy is, then employees could be pulling in different potentially non-strategic directions. Putting a balanced scorecard on the desktops of employees is a way to ensure that they are exposed to performance issues and how their day-to day decisions may affect these according to McCann (2000).

In building a scorecard, an organization will go through the process of creating a new way of managing. Areas which are likely to be assessed will include clarifying and agreeing strategy, educating (or re-educating) the organization, aligning business processes throughout the company and introducing a feedback system. A team of people who will be instrumental in the implementation can be organized. This is not like implementing ABM or total quality management which are more focused. The team should spend time discussing and reaching a consensus on what the company's vision is, identifying strategic issues and how they can be understood and communicated to the rest of the company. It is imperative that scorecard development has the commitment and attention of senior executives. There are three critical roles for the team:

- **A designer who takes ownership of the project, educates the**

executive team and turns strategy into action;
- For a scorecard to be effectively implemented, it should be endorsed by a senior member of the company;
- An individual should be responsible for ensuring the aims of the scorecard are understood throughout the rest of the organization.

Strategic objectives are the foundation of any scorecard, so their identification is a key step in implementation. The designer will need to gather information on areas such as competitors, trends in market size and growth, customers and current and future technology innovations. These can then be considered in the context of the four perspectives developed by Kaplan and Norton (1996).

Once the new strategy is decided, it should be communicated to the middle managers in the organization. This should involve the people who constitute the top three layers of management. Strategy should be discussed with them to ensure that the way forward is clear. Projects, programmes or initiatives that do not reflect the new corporate strategy, should be eliminated.

The finalised corporate scorecard should be used as a basis for allowing each business unit to formulate its own objectives targets and strategy. Strategic business units will all have their own products, customers and communication channels. Mission and strategy statements should be established for each department, taking into account their individual needs and aims, but always linking them back to the corporate scorecard. The balanced scorecard should become part of the management process and highlight possibilities to link individual objectives and financial reward back into the scorecard.

Balanced Scorecards Can Fail!

Although the balanced scorecard can offer a variety of benefits as identified by Kaplan and Norton (2002), implementing the technique is not without problems. Some commentators have reported for a long time instances of failure. As high as 70 per cent of balanced scorecard implementations fail (see McCunn, 1998). McCunn has identified ten 'commandments' of balanced scorecard implementation (see Table 5.2).

Rousseau and Rousseau (2000) note further pitfalls in the implementation of a balanced scorecard. They suggest that since the balanced scorecard concept is normally introduced from the top down, the organization often starts with the development of its first scorecard at the top level of the organization. The selected measures are therefore applicable to the executive committee and the senior management team. Although this scorecard can be considered the management cockpit of the organization, when it is not followed by the development of multiple linked balanced scorecards that ultimately connect to the individual employee. According to these authors, for strategy to be realised successfully, it must be translated into actions. Moreover, it should involve people at all levels of the organization, not just at the top.

Table 5.2 Ten Commandments of the Balanced Scorecard

Do ...	In Other Words ...
– Use the scorecard as an implementation pad for strategic goals;	– it can be an ideal vehicle for rolling the corporate strategy down through the organization.
– Ensure strategic goals are in place before the scorecard is implemented;	– do not invent the strategy as you go along, or the scorecard will drive the wrong behaviour.
– Ensure that a top-level (non-financial) sponsor backs the scorecard and that relevant line managers are committed to the project;	– the scorecard project is too big to be anything other than top priority, and it should never be left to the accountants to do.
– Implement a pilot before introducing the new scorecard;	– it provides valuable lessons and avoids 'big bang' risks.
– Carry out an 'entry review' for each business unit before implementing the scorecard.	– this minimises the risk of going ahead in unfavourable circumstances and allows one to customise the project to suit the organization's needs.
Do Not ...	
– Use the scorecard to obtain extra top-down control.	– people will rebel.
– Attempt to standardise the project. The scorecard must e tailor-made;	– the organization's strategic imperatives are unique – a ready-made scorecard will not fit.
– Underestimate the need for training and communication in using the scorecard.	– do not be fooled by the simplicity of the idea – one has to deal with the huge change it brings.
– Seek complexity nor strive for perfection.	– avoid 'paralysis by analysis'.
– Underestimate the extra administrative workload and costs of periodic scorecard reporting.	– gathering information for the scorecard is more time-consuming than one might expect.

(Source: McCunn, 1998)

The performance measures of a balanced scorecard are sometimes mapped to the value drivers of the financial institution or the subsection of it to which the scorecard relates. Moreover, the sensitivity of the value drivers can be used to select those performance measures that relate to the value drivers which create the most value for any given improvement.

A balanced scorecard is sometimes developed and integrated into the reporting process, which continues to report as usual, but on different measures. Performance measures are more than just about reporting. Each performance measure might need a target, defined actions to reach this target, and an owner to lead the implementation of these actions. The difference between performance reporting and performance management needs to be clearly identified (Rousseau and Rousseau, 2000). Generally, to be accepted, the form and substance of a performance measurement system needs to be understood by its users and needs to fit the culture and operational context of the enterprise. This is no different of the implementation of any management accounting technique.

Some commentators hold that performance measures should seek to facilitate decision and actions that support strategies based on the needs of stakeholders. These stakeholders include stockholders, internal and external customers, regulatory bodies, managers and employees. The goal is to encourage the wider adoption of this link and the development of better quantitative performance measures as well as supplementary qualitative performance indicators. Performance measures can monitor quantitative variables (e.g., a direct measure of lead time) or serve as proxies for qualitative variables (e.g., employees' turnover rates to help monitor trends in employee morale). Performance indicators can also monitor qualitative variables (e.g., a consultant's assessment of the level of employee morale as high, moderate, or low) or represent quantitative variables (e.g., a manager's evaluation of lead time as satisfactory or unsatisfactory).

Performance measurement systems have altered alongside changes in operational technologies including the shift from labour intensive production to the adoption of automated and flexible technologies. The shift has been accompanied by a growing awareness that non-financial monitors matter and that systems designers must understand both technical and operational processes as well as organizational, behavioural and cultural factors. Ultimately, managers have a desire to monitor relevant performance measures as much as they seek to prioritise cost determination in pursuit of organizational excellence.

The Balance Scorecard and Risk Management

Organizations face risks in the course of implementing strategy or altering their operations. Risk can be defined as the likelihood that some factor or event will prevent an organization from achieving its objectives. An important question is: would it be possible to take the balanced scorecard and integrate it with risk management to link strategy management *and* risk management? We can think of the balance between value creation through strategy implementation and the avoidance of value destruction, as risk management. As noted in this book, strategic finance helps explicitly incorporate the concept of risk and return into the strategy management process. It is possible to expand the "balance" concept in a way that can extend the usefulness of the balanced scorecard according to Nagumo and Donlon (2006).

Increasingly, risk management is a priority for firms because risk is a ubiquitous concern that has to be faced by all enterprises. Moreover, risk and strategy are interlinked. A clearly defined strategy is required for an appropriate risk management function. The presence of appropriate risk management sets the boundaries for the strategy to be pursued.

To illustrate the relationships between strategy implementation and risk, Nagumo and Donlon (2006) take an example of a strategy for increasing revenue and a strategy for productivity, which are classic strategic themes to which the balanced scorecard is applied. First, consider the risk scenario for a "increase revenue" strategy. As one pursued by profit-seeking organizations, this strategy often consists of entering new business territories through corporate acquisition, direct foreign investment to penetrate new markets, targeting a new customer segment, and launching new products. In addition to external marketing activities, typically this strategy must be promoted internally from a managerial perspective and often involves getting personnel to be more results-oriented. When considering the implications of implementing this strategy, the following risks must be addressed:

- Business failure due to management's lack of know-how about the new business area
- Sudden increase in country risk due to deterioration of conditions in the target country

- Failure of new product development due to unanticipated changes in customer preferences
- Morale issues and brain drain due to hastily implemented results-oriented policies
- Increased profit volatility as a result of any of the risks in this list

The balanced scorecard may not be designed to manage these risks. The conventional methodology for implementing the balanced scorecard does not address the issue of risk management in these terms. It is possible to think about the relationship between strategy and risk management and integrating them into the balanced scorecard by examining the Committee of the Sponsoring Organization for the Treadway Commission (COSO) Enterprise Risk Management (ERM) framework according to these authors. The COSO ERM is a three-dimensional model consisting of four management objectives, eight components of risk management, and the organizational units.

The model systematically analyzes the risk that accompanies implementation of a strategy, and manages the risk to a tolerable level. In this manner, the similarities between COSO ERM and the balanced scorecard can be visualised. When the COSO ERM management objectives are examined, they are almost the same as the areas covered by the internal process perspective of the balanced scorecard. Strategy corresponds to what is covered in the balanced scorecard's strategic themes such as product leadership, complete customer solutions, low cost operations, and system lock-in. Operations here refers to "strategy" cascaded down to the operational level. Reporting corresponds to financial reporting, corporate social responsibility (CSR) reporting, communication with shareholders, authorities, and external stakeholders, and building a brand image. Compliance corresponds to the basic requirements in terms of regulatory compliance for good corporate citizenship.

The internal environment indicates how the management team perceives the importance of risk management. This corresponds to the balanced scorecard's goal to mobilize change through executive leadership which is one of the principles of the strategy-focused organization. Objective setting corresponds to clarifying strategy, which is a primary balanced scorecard function addressed through the strategy mapping activity. There is nothing corresponding to event identification, risk assessment, risk response, and control activities: Which are at the heart of COSO ERM risk management. In COSO ERM, information and communication means that information needed for risk management freely flows vertically and horizontally within the organization; the balanced scorecard seeks to ensure that strategic information is cascaded from the top and feedback flows back up from employees. In COSO ERM, monitoring is typically conducted by two parties: management and internal auditors. Management monitors organizational unit performance versus the strategy using the balanced scorecard.

There are numerous issues that require careful thinking if an enterprise is to implement the balanced scorecard linked with enterprise risk management. The balanced scorecard and COSO ERM are in some firms becoming established as formal mechanisms to deal with strategy and risk management.

6

STRATEGY MATTERS

The same year that Michael Dell founded his company, 1984, Liu Chuanzhi founded his business which eventually would become Lenovo. In 1995, Lenovo purchased IBM's money losing PC business, quickly turning it around and making it the second largest PC maker in 2012 with a 13.4% market share compared to Dell's 10.1%. Dell's strategy has always been one of cost leadership. Lenovo's strategy has been to price products aggressively at first scarifying margins and seeking profits only after the market share gets into double digits. Lenovo seeks to offer products which blur the the lines between product types – a strategy of 'netbookization and iPadization of the PC' (27/6/2011 Time p. 51). The company also crosses traditionally distinct corporate strategies: In January 2013, Lenovo reorganised itself setting up Lenovo Business Group to make PCs for cost conscious consumers and the Think Business Group for premium customers to compete with Apple. Lenovo's view of the future of the PC and of corporate strategy pursuit remains contrarian.

Strategy and Planning

Management thinkers almost universally regard planning as being fundamental to the effective management of an enterprise. Planning broadly encompasses choosing objectives, identifying various ways of achieving goals and deciding on a set of actions which may then be monitored and controlled. Planning is underpinned by action about possible action. It is thus closely tied to control. Management control aims at ensuring that resources are obtained and used effectively and efficiently to realise organizational objectives as indicated by the strategic plan. Many managers continue to subscribe to this definition which was first proposed by Harvard Business School academic Robert Anthony in 1965. Whilst efficiency is viewed as an important element of planning and control, many industries have been considered to have become more efficient but without evidence that individual companies within those industries have become more profitable. Effectiveness is thus important as it suggest movement in the right direction. Direction in turn is established by strategy.

Strategising in terms of the above suggests building the company's strategic direction for the future and designing the business model that is intended to deliver superior performance. Hamel (1996) has described several routes to industry 'revolution' as the basis for strategizing:

- **re-conceiving the product or service: radically improving the value equation;**

- redefining market space: pushing the bounds of universality;

- **redrawing industry boundaries: rescaling industries such as taking a local business national or making a larger business global; compressing the supply chain; driving convergence across industries.**

Strategy may be regarded as a logic underlying an organization's interaction with its environment, which in turn influences its deployment of resources. But an extension of this is sometimes evident when managers are observed as they engage in operational activities which link to some longer term objective. This perspective may be regarded as "descriptive". The view portrays strategy as complex in its interaction between management, employees and the environment and as existing in a state of flux with consequences that are loosely tied to those aims being pursued. Here strategy is organizationally grounded whereby enterprise activities are shaped by diverse interests, institutional pressures and diffuse webs of decision-making. The task for managers within this perspective is to create a context for strategy formation and to detect patterns that emerge and help them to take shape (Mintzberg, 1976). Information sources are seen as being diverse and only partially derived from formalised systems. The communication of information sources affecting strategic processes is non-uniform and information flows and formats can be extensively unstructured (Goold and Quinn, 1990).

At an opposite extreme, a "prescriptive" view regards strategy as a formalised statement of intent which identifies objectives and intended actions. Enterprises are regarded as engaging in strategic choice making in an economically rational manner within the constraints of limited information, cognitive biases and a lack of knowledge as to cause and effect in organizational matters. Strategy is here seen as consciously identified, proactive and formulated prior to decisions and actions. This view is espoused by Porter (1985, 1999) whose notion of competitive differentiation has influenced financial control thinking extensively. Porter (1999) does not see strategy as a search simply for internal efficiencies in the company, or even the supply chain, but as a focus on the general management responsibility for <u>strategic positioning</u>. This underscores the need to define the value provided to customers, compared to competitors, as the basis of competitive advantage and superior performance.

Competitive differentiation

Effective strategy is regarded within the prescriptive view as relying on clear competitive differentiation exploiting the core competencies of a business. Value is created by carrying out key activities that competitors cannot readily replicate. For instance Amazon.com establishes core strengths tied to its fulfillment and delivery capacity which become blended with brand name, trust and publicity which cannot easily be replicated by its competitors.

The best-known approach to considering competitive differentiation is that provided by Porter (1985). Porter believes that in spite of the apparent complexity of competitive strategy there are two sources of competitive advantage: low cost and differentiation. This leads to the identification of three generic strategies, as illustrated in Figure 6.1.

Porter's view of an enterprise's competitive choice is that it can compete on a broad or narrow scope, being either a price leader or a differentiator. A firm has to avoid the danger of becoming a 'stuck in the middle' company which will be unable to compete effectively. Groups of competitors may be positioned in terms of their strategies. For instance, one might be able to categorise the complex market for personal writing instruments into

- **broad scope / price leadership: cheaper brands (eg: Primark, Lidl)**
- **broad scope / differentiators: mass-market brands (eg: Hollister, Gap, Mexx etc.) which are differentiated by**

branding, design, packaging, and so on;
- narrow scope / price leadership: own-label clothing, badged hotel clothing (eg: George);
- narrow scope / differentiators: exclusive brands (eg: Prada, Armani)

Figure 6.1. Porter's generic strategies

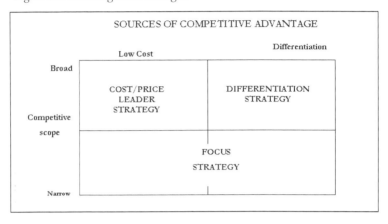

> A company can outperform rivals only if it can establish a difference that it can preserve. It must deliver greater value to customers or create comparable value at a lower cost, or do both. The arithmetic of superior profitability then follows: delivering greater value allows a company to charge higher unit prices; greater efficiency results in lower average unit costs (Porter, 1998, p. 294)

This view raises three significant questions in building a strategy:
- **What differences can an organization establish or exploit in the market?**
- **In what ways do these differences represent superior value to all or some customers in the market?**
- **Can this form of differentiation be sustained and defend against 'me-too' imitations by existing or new competitors?**

Increasingly, the sustainability of competitive advantage is proving difficult to achieve for many enterprises. Both the speed of change in the market and the ability of competitors to identify and meet customer demands are creating entirely new challenges for market players.

Competitive Forces

Strategy may be considered as guiding different organizational initiatives and determining which management approaches a company should use. With intense competition across international markets, internet technologies making global business activities more viable and competitively more fierce and shortening product lifecycles, companies seek to analyse carefully the competitive forces that affect existing and emerging lines of business. Using Porter's (1985, 1998, 2001) model, competitive forces can be assessed in terms of threats include those posed by

- **Competitors**
- **New entrants**
- **Substitution**
- **Bargaining power of buyers and**
- **Bargaining power of suppliers**

For high-technology companies and many service based industries, the threat from competitors and the threat of substitution can create tremendous pressures to develop new products and to rapidly bring them to market. At the broadest level, companies examine competitive pressures for each line of business and formulate strategic responses for each line. These responses (as discussed in other sections of this book) can include the following:

- **Development of new products**
- **Expansion of market niches**
- **Automation and investment in manufacturing systems**
- **Investment in information technology**
- **Enhancement of quality**
- **Enhancement of customer satisfaction.**

Companies can, on occasion, formulate strategic responses based on core competencies which can form the roots of competitive advantage. Often, companies invest in new technology or development to strengthen their core competencies. These can then be leveraged to rapidly develop new products in several different lines of business rapidly.

Once a strategic response has been formulated following the analysis of competitive forces and core competencies, tools such as total quality management and activity analysis can be used to facilitate rapid implementation of strategy. According to Ray (1995), the type and mix of tools varies depending on the line of business and the chosen strategic response.

Core competencies

Prahalad and Hamel (1990) have proposed a specific view of the 'core competence of the corporation', which can be combined with the model of competitive differentiation and positioning. They question how an organization can differentiate effectively if it does not understand its capabilities. The focus has to be on how an organization addresses the issue of value to the customer, and the marketing assets the firm has at its disposal to create the value which underpins competitive positioning.

Prahalad and Hamel (1990) have examined the characteristics of companies that have succeeded in investing in new markets and the dramatically shifting patterns of customer choices in established markets. They conclude that the common characteristic is that these companies understand, exploit, invest to create, and sustain core competencies. Examples include:

- **Apple: the ability to style technology**
- **Sony: the capacity to miniaturise**
- **Philips: optical-media expertise**
- **Citicorp: competence in systems**
- **3M: competence with sticky tape**
- **Black and Decker: expertise with small electrical motors**
- **Canon: skills in optics, imaging and microprocessors**
- **Casio: competence in display systems.**
- **Starbucks: the ability to create consumer experience from consumption**

These characteristics are viewed as the most basic corporate resources, which lead to success in apparently diverse markets and products, and suggest that even the largest of companies are unlikely to have more than five or six core competencies (Donelan and Kaplan, 1998). Consider for instance Zappos.com. A few years ago the idea of selling something as tactile and personal as shoes over the internet seemed unlikely as a business model. Zappos.com holds a fifth of the online footwear market with 4 million customers and over $1 billion in revenues. The CEO Tony Hsieh made the return process the company's core competitive advantage. The ease of return makes Zappos shopper 75% repeat customers. Mr Hsieh has established long-term customer retention as its "key strategy". Prepaid return shipping is the gateway to achieving that strategy.

Piercy (1999) suggests that companies need to carefully consider which of their core capabilities are valuable in particular markets. Questions that may be asked include:

- **Does this capability create value for the customer in this market?** If not, it is of no use in developing a strategy for this market.
- **Will competitors find it hard to copy this capability? If every company can replicate this, there is no competitive advantage.**
- **What is the probable duration of the uniqueness? How long does the company have before the competition can catch up?**
- **Who is the primary beneficiary of the capability? Does it relate to particular segments of the market on which the company should focus?**
- **Does another capability satisfy the same market need? Does the organization face competition from substitution?**
- **Is the firm's core capability really superior to the competition?**

Ultimately strategic strength may be seen to come from competitive differentiation – doing the things that matter in the market different to competitors, or doing different things – which exploits a company's core competencies. The idea of "differentiating capabilities" combines these two approaches – the issue is what activities an organization does better than the rest, and which create superior value for customers.

An established approach to identifying a business's capabilities (and corresponding weaknesses) and relating these to opportunities and threats in the outside world is SWOT analysis (*S*trengths, *W*eaknesses, *O*pportunities and *T*hreats). It provides a simple, but structured, approach to evaluating a company's strategic position. In evaluating a company's strengths and weaknesses, only those resources or capabilities which would be recognised and valued by the customer should be included. The same approach can be used to view the opportunities and threats in the environment – the specific market, customer, issue, etc. Consider for instance pencils made by Faber-Castell since 1876 which were recently seen to be under threat of becoming undervalued and undifferentiated. Head of the firm Count Anton Wolfgang von Faber-Castell believes that his pencils are the best in the world. One day he threw 144 of them out of the window. They fell 30 metres onto hard tarmac – and none broke. The graphite lead is so firmly squeezed and glued into its pinewood sleeve that it will not shatter unlike pencils of lesser brands.

Pencil-making might appear to be a commodity business - surely one pencil is much like another? But Count Faber-Castell considers that this is not so and that traditional writing tools still have a place in the internet era. The computer has not yet eclipsed the humble pencil: there is no substitute for the cheapness and practicality of coloured and graphite pencils for children, artists, office workers, designers, and the billions of people without computers. Faber-Castell's continued branding of their pencils as non-commodities as a successful strategy. The firm has factories at 16 sites worldwide, including Peru, Indonesia, India and China, and makes 2 billion pencils a year (The Economist 3/3/07 p78).

It is important to recognise that opportunities and threats exist only in the outside world – the things one might propose to do about them are the strategies. For example, it may be suggested that price-cutting is an opportunity. This is not an opportunity in a SWOT analysis – it is a price tactic which one might adopt. One would only accept the desirability of price-cutting if, for example, the company's size gave it greater cost economies than its competitors, and that there was an identified, external market opportunity in terms of there being a price-sensitive segment of the market, or the need to meet a competitor's threatened entry to the market with low prices.

One recurring observation of successful organizations is that strategy is often embedded in change which itself is not usually predictable. The corporate world has many examples of individuals driving such change - whether it is Jeff Bezos at Amazon.com, Norbert Reithofer at BMW, Cyrus Mistry at Tata, or Alhaji Aliko Dangote of Dangote Group - these individuals have a sense of purpose, which makes the unconventional happen. Their vision may not always be shared across their organization. For instance, the emergence of Sony's Playstation products and its focus on digital as opposed to analog technology emerged from the conviction of one individual running a renegade operation until top management support for the strategy finally ensued. Likewise, SAP AG was founded in 1972 by five German engineers with IBM in Mannheim, Germany. When an IBM client asked IBM to provide enterprise-wide software to run on its mainframe, the five began writing the program only to be told the assignment was being transferred to another unit. Rather than abandon the project altogether, they left IBM and founded SAP. It has become the world's largest business software company. Thus strategic change is often unpredictable and core competencies will shift over time.

Consider also the Marriott hotel group: Marriott hired IDEO Inc. to rethink the hotel experience for an increasingly important customer: the young, tech-savvy road warrior. "This is all about looking freshly at business travel and how people behave and what they need." (Michael Jannini, Marriott's executive vice-president for brand management). To better understand Marriott's customers, IDEO dispatched a team of seven consultants, including a designer, anthropologist, writer, and architect, on a six-week trip. Covering 12 cities, the group hung out in hotel lobbies, cafes, and bars, and asked guests to graph what they were doing our by hour. They learned that hotels are generally good at serving large parties but not so much at small groups of business travelers. Researchers found that hotel lobbies tend to be dark and better suited to killing time than conducting casual business. Marriott lacked places where guest could comfortably combine work with pleasure outside their rooms.

Having studied IDEO's findings, Marriott is now reinventing the lobbies of its Marriott and Renaissance hotels, creating for each a social zone, with small tables, brighter lights, and wireless Web access - all better suited to meetings. Solo travelers will be able to work or unwind in larger, quiet, semiprivate spaces where they do not have to worry about spilling coffee on their laptops or papers (S. Ante, "The science of desire Business Week 5/6/05 p101-106).

The argument has been made that the source of strategic advantage is never a constant. Once the source of strategic strength becomes widely available – it ceases to be of strategic value. Carr (2003) notes that whereas information technology (IT) was at one stage a possible source of strategic value for many enterprises, it now no longer is. IT has become a commodity. As its power and ubiquity has grown, its strategic importance has diminished. Carr (2003, p. 10) remarks that: "IT management should, frankly, become boring. The key to success, for the vast majority of companies is no longer to seek advantage aggressively but to manage costs and risks meticulously".

Why Do Strategies Fail?

Corboy and O'Corrbui (1999) identify a number of pitfalls which may militate against desired strategy implementation. They state that up to 70 per cent of business strategies fail to get implemented and that strategy is of limited value unless it is acted upon. Strategy implementation moreover has a poor track record. Corboy and O'Corrbui (1999) note that this is often the result of an organization committing one or more of 'the seven deadly sins of strategy implementation':

The strategy is not worth implementing: This occurs where business strategy is deficient in analytical rigour, creative insight, ambition or practicality. The strategy represents just more of what has happened previously with no enhanced sense of vision or challenge for the organization.

People are not clear how the strategy will be implemented: When the strategy has been developed and evaluated, a plan may be considered necessary to prepare the organization for its implementation. But there may be a number of issues which need to be addressed first, including:

Priorities: what are the organizational priorities? Which parts of the strategy should be implemented first? Have these priorities been made clear?

Timescale: how quickly is it intended that the strategy be implemented? Is it feasible to do it in that timeframe?

Lessons learnt: what can be learned from previous experiences of strategy implementation?

Impact: what impact or implications will the strategy have on customers and employees and on existing organizational activities?

Participation: who needs to be involved and when? Have they got what it takes to make it work?

Risks: what are the risks which might prevent the firm from implementing the strategy and can these risks be managed?

Customers and staff do not fully understand the strategy: This is a problem which may hinder other aspects of organizational functioning. Communication may be key to addressing this concern.

Individual responsibilities for implementing the change are not clear: Developing a very insightful and relevant strategy in the hope that the logic behind the strategy will be enough to make it a reality may not suffice. Often, individuals need to be given clear and specific responsibilities for making the strategy work.

Senior managers step out of the picture once implementation begins: As is the case with any organizational activity which affects a large segment of individuals or resources, top management support and involvement is essential.

The 'brick walls' are not recognised: Unforeseen events or difficulties tend to arise during implementation. It is important that obstacles are acknowledged and addressed.

Forgetting to 'mind the shop': At times, the process of developing and implementing strategy can become the all-consuming concern of senior management. The operational priority is to run the organization and meet targets to provide services and serve customers. Strategy should be seen as a means rather than an end in itself.

Whilst these seven 'deadly sins' seem apparent, they are not always heeded. Of equal significance is to assume that strategy development is a deliberate and purposive activity. In many, organizations it is described an <u>emergent</u> rather than a <u>deliberate</u> process (Mintzberg, Quinn and Ghoshal, 1999). Instead of being formulated, strategy may be seen as undergoing formation without express articulation (Lynch, 2000). As such, imposing excessive functional structure and defined rationality to processes which defy such characterisation is inappropriate. As noted above some writers on strategy take a <u>prescriptive</u> and normative view advocating very particular and usually simplistic ways in which to engage in strategic management. By contrast, others take a <u>descriptive</u> view based on their reflections on how strategic processes are played out in organizations (see Table 6.1).

Table 6.1 Conceptions of Strategy

The Prescriptive View	The Descriptive View
- Proactive	- Complex
- Sequential	- Dynamic
- Linear	- Multi-level
- Focus on Formulation	- Focus on Formation
- Structured	- Emergent
More suited to order?	More suited to chaos?

Mintzberg (1978) has drawn a distinction between intended and realized strategies. The former refers to intended actions identified in a formal mission statement. Strategy is as described above, viewed as being objectively formulated before decisions are made so intent and actions can be aligned. Realized strategies emerge via environmental interactions and events on an ongoing basis over time. Thus intended strategy may not be realized and realized strategies may be unintended.

Strategic Controls

Control systems are sometimes expected to accomplish the impossible: plan for uncertain conditions and monitor outcomes under complex operating conditions. Control systems may be deemed successful when they assist an organization to accomplish its strategic pursuits. An adequate fit between the methods used to control daily operations and the overall strategic direction of the company may need to be in place whilst changing customer needs and emerging product developments are assessed. Management accounting systems are often regarded as one form of management control. When strategic analysis becomes embedded within such systems, they become powerful tools for pursuing longer term managerial objectives.

Strategic management accounting (SMA) is a term which captures links between cost management and strategic issues which many senior accounting executives view as increasingly important. SMA entails the preparation and presentation of information for decision-making, placing especial emphasis on external factors and forward looking concerns. The focus is on business strategy as affected by levels and trends in real costs and prices, volume, market share, cash flow and the demands made on a firm's total resources. The basis of such a view is that information affects strategy and conceptions of strategy must, in turn, affect the way in which information is constructed, presented and used. It follows that since individual organizations develop their own individual strategies, they must determine their own particular approach to determining the structure of SMA information.

There is presently only a very small body of literature that directly addresses the relationship between management accounting and corporate strategy; no agreed comprehensive conceptual framework for strategic management accounting currently exists according to Roslender and Hart (2003). Cravens and Guilding (2001, p.98) note that "The absence of a literature concerned with distilling what practices comprise SMA is striking".

Strategic control criteria

Various steps are involved in taking a strategic approach to producing management accounting based control information. The following form a potential sequence identified by Simmonds (1988, 1989).

(1) Develop a dynamic view of strategic business units:
The idea of a strategic business unit (SBU) cannot be fixed and permanent, it must be identified at a particular time. The management accounting system can be redesigned so as to de-emphasise traditionally determined responsibility centres and to stimulate management to consider what might be appropriate units for strategic action. For this to take place there must be an acceptance of strategic competitive position as the determinant for identifying units. At the SBU level, there must be a concern for areas of the external environment which are critical to the achievement of its goals and objectives. Planning resources should be concentrated on these critical success factors and business strategies should be selected accordingly.

One approach is to consider Porter's value chain as discussed above. The value chain looks at the total value added by the industry and by the particular organization within that industry. The contribution of each primary and support activity carried out by the organization can then be separated. The activities which are identified to add most significantly to the total value added are focused upon. Certainly, this is of fundamental importance in cost management terms, but it also enables strategies to be developed to improve or defend the existing share of the value-added from which the enterprise benefits. Figure 6.2 depicts Porter's value chain.

Figure 6.2 Porter's value chain

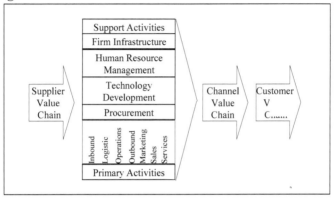

Shank and Govindarajan (1996) have placed considerable weight on Porter's notion of strategic positioning. To them, a value chain perspective on strategic cost management requires that firms recognise their product in the total value-creating chain of activities, and that they endeavour to develop accounting information that enables improvement of internal cost management performance. The emphasis, then, is not simply on competition, but also on the interaction that firms have with their suppliers.

(2)   Strategic achievement comes from relative performance:

Profit comes from competing effectively. The strategy focuses on how to achieve this. Strategic success is about relative performance. On its own, internal cost efficiency is not enough for success. Volume, market share or accumulated experience also do not suffice. If the strategy produces relative success and profits, further expansion will follow profitability and bring with it increase in relative volume, relative market share or relative accumulated experience. To provide management with strategy guidance, all indicators must thus be measured in terms of relative position against specified competitors.

Beyond the need for internal information that managers consider useful is the need to more clearly understand the competitive situation. Finance professionals need to provide their companies with competitor cost and strategic information in addition to the information provided on internal operations. Consider for instance how <u>competitor cost analysis</u> has been implemented at Caterpillar, Inc. in the USA whose continuing objective is to be the lowest-cost, highest-value producer in the industry. Before undertaking factory modernisation, the competitive situation was analysed from perspectives of price, cost, industry capacity and competitor strategies. This effort resulted in the establishment of a total company-wide structural cost reduction target and individual product-by-product targets. These targets provide the impetus for strategies for modernising manufacturing operations and reducing costs, and provide the benchmarks against which the unfolding improvements are monitored.

A key aspect of competitor analysis concerns the point at which a competitor's cost advantage is large enough that it cannot be eliminated through evolutionary or 'business as usual' cost reduction efforts. When a manufacturer's cost problems are beyond that point, revolutionary change may be required.

The simplest form of analysis would be to divide a competitor's costs from the published financial statements by the units produced and determine an average product cost. This, however, would not yield very useful information for trying to analyse the cost of complex, multi-product manufacturers. At the other end of the spectrum would be the ideal: the development of very specific product cost estimates based on detailed information about the competitor's cost structure, products and the product's costs in the production process. This information is, understandably, not available. Therefore, available published information is used as the basis for analyses which, of course, have significant limitations.

Obtaining reliable internal product costs is regarded as a prerequisite for competitor cost analysis. If a company's own product cost system cannot meet this test then competitor evaluation will be of little value. For the company with an appropriate product costing system, however, competitor analysis can be an insightful tool for maintaining or gaining competitive advantage.

The first step in a competitive study is to establish overall objectives with specific estimates of the costs of competitor's products and some insight into competitor strategies, practices and plans. This requires an intensive

information-gathering process possibly using multi-functional teams. A macro plan might be developed as follows:
- Gather published information that could include: history, financial, products, sales/volumes, marketing/distribution/service, manufacturing facilities and processes, governmental relationships, strategies, value engineering, cost reduction, quality control, labour relations and people levels, technology/product design, organization, and suppliers/purchased material.
- Use public information sources such as: annual reports, product and plant brochures, financial analysts reports, seminars and symposia, industry sales/volumes reports, trade journals and published articles, governmental agencies and industry statistical publications.
- Gather information through techniques including multi-functional teams to study manufacturing and sourcing methods; analyse competitor's products from design, quality, processing and material sourcing perspectives.
- Assess the information. Lift from it the portions which will provide the means of establishing cost models.
- Formulate product cost estimates using several approaches as a means of cross-checking and testing the answers which will ultimately be used.
- Test the aggregated final product cost estimates against the adjusted 'cost of goods sold' from the annual report to see if the answers are acceptably close.
- Compare competitor product cost estimates with individual in-house product costs once the estimates are judged to be acceptable.
- Arrive at an aggregated product cost difference by extending the competitor cost estimates by in-house volumes and product mix and compare with in-house aggregated costs calculated the same way.
- Analyse and quantify future competitor cost reduction programmes.
- Add to the individual product cost and aggregated cost differences any estimates of future competitor cost reductions.
- Include the cost effects of freight and duty or any other non-product-related costs if applicable.

- Adjust for value differences to complete the study. Business strategies such as distribution systems, product and parts support, product quality, product differentiation and product capabilities to be analysed as to benefit provided. A comparison to be made with the competing company's benefit yield from its various business strategies and a value advantage/disadvantage to be determined thereby. An aggregated cost profile may take the form below.
- Establish company-wide strategies to reduce costs to targeted levels.

The illustration below shows some possible information elements related to competitor cost which can be included in managerial reports and which will provoke continuous strategic analysis.

Our product costs	100
Competitor product costs	80
Gross product cost difference	20
Future competitor cost reduction	5
	25
Our freight and duty advantage	(8)
Our value advantage	(5)
Net total cost disadvantage	12

The difficulty of the task, analysis methods and approaches, and quality of results will vary by company. The task of analysis becomes more difficult if the competitor:
- is in other, unrelated businesses;
- has abnormal and non-recurring costs buried in its cost structure;
- has a different organizational structure;
- has factories located in other countries;
- has different levels of vertical integration;
- segregates costs differently for public reports;
- produces other products (not directly competitive);
- produces product, service parts, modified products and other non-standard products which are all lumped together in the cost structure; and
- produces different volumes and mix of products.

Value differences should be assessed and included in the report. This is because one company could have a product cost advantage over another but could lose that advantage if the costs of merchandising and supporting its products were considerably higher, or if the quality or capabilities of its products were inferior.

Comparative value or productivity judgements, although usually more subjective than product cost comparisons, can be a desirable element in assessing the overall cost differences between two competing companies. These elements can be referred to as a cost advantage or disadvantage. That is, a competitor may not be able to overcome these advantages with lower product costs. If the competitor wanted to negate these advantages it could increase its own costs in order to do so. Consequently, competitor analysis considers any possible value differences and includes an estimate of the cost implications. Once this adjustment is made, along with other adjustments for freight, duty and future cost reduction estimates – comparisons can be made to in-house costs as shown in Table 6.2.

Determining the total estimated cost structure difference (for the products being compared) requires that competitor unit costs be extended by in-house volumes and product mix, and compared with total in-house costs calculated the same way. This aggregated cost calculation generates the total structural cost differences. The product-by-product differences can be shown and a total cost difference provided.

The costing results could be augmented with detailed information as to which operational differences and elements of costs are causing the major differences and why. The strategic information may provide a clearer understanding of competition from key perspectives, including an assessment of future strategies.

Table 6.2. Product cost structure comparisons

Product	Our cost £	Their cost £	Cost reduction targets £	% reduction needed
A	12,500	10,000	2,500	20
B	13,000	12,000	1,000	8
C	17,000	15,000	2,000	12
D	22,500	20,000	2,500	11
E	10,000	8,000	2,000	20
F	28,500	25,000	3,500	12
G	14,500	13,000	1,500	10
H	10,000	9,000	1,000	10

(3) Present value of the business is an overriding objective:

Strategic performance is measured by change in the present value of the net cash flow that can be extracted from a business. When this change is added to or subtracted from the accounting profit for a period, it provides an estimate of economic performance over the period. As an objective for business, maximisation of present value ties current performance and the future value of competitive position together. If adequate recognition is not given to change in the present value of competitive position, there may be a tendency to impair competitive position to gain current accounting profits. This is clearly not acceptable if it decreases the overall present value. With SMA the emphasis may be moved from performance measurement based on period accounting profit on its own, to performance measurement using at least some indicators of competitive position.

(4) Short-run cost variation is paramount:

When strategic reversals happen, they happen in the present. Firms seldom meet their current capacity exactly, and the short-term cost implications of variation from optimal are usually quite major. In many mature industries such as motor vehicles, television manufacturing and bicycles, competitors have come from smaller volume bases to overtake firms with huge accumulated experience. The experienced company will have been forced up a short-term cost curve that is much steeper than the long-term volume or experience curves. Once begun, retrenchment is difficult to reverse. Retrenchment becomes retreat and retreat rout, as the short-term cost curve gets steeper and steeper and financial resources are drained (Simmonds, 1989).

(5) Financial practices are changed radically:

If each business unit in a firm adopts a strategy so as to maximise its present value, the firm's total present value can only be increased by some broad strategy that increases its value more than that of a competitor. The overall present value is not increased by taking more cash from one business unit to decrease its present value and giving it to another business unit. Portfolio adjustment solely as an internal cash-balancing process based on differential returns on investment would be a zero-sum game.

Under SMA, investment in each business unit is justified solely in terms of the strategy that maximises present value. Investment in the total firm is the sum of the investment in the individual businesses. The financial policy of the firm is thus derived from the business strategies rather than vice versa.

This approach runs contrary to a common financial approach of budgeting cash flow plus overall debt increase and then allocating this sum to businesses on the basis of return on investment. Such an approach also negates the commonly held view that return comes from the physical manifestations of capital such as plant, buildings, stock, etc. Physical assets become only the means to building competitive strength. Having a plant does not in itself produce profits if the competitive position it supports does not put the firm in a profit-earning position.

Implementation Issues

The ideas underlying strategic control are not new to all enterprises. SMA-type information is often utilised when defending the enterprise against a hostile bid or considering a takeover bid where, for example, using whatever information can be obtained, the buying firm seeks to evaluate the promise of the attributes possessed by the candidate firm's products and to determine any cost advantages this firm possesses or could possess in providing these attributes.

Strategic controls incorporate strategic product costing and performance measurement, analyses of the firm's product markets and competitive market forces, and the assessment of organizational strategies over extended periods of time. Implementing such controls entails extensive managerial effort. Consider the example of Goldstar Electronics, a major Korean electronics firm which adopts strategic control procedures when planning for those projects fundamental to the company's success but about which the company lacks detailed information. Goldstar's first step in appraising such projects is to determine what are called environmental factors in the company's planning process. This involves answering detailed questions including:

- **What are the uses of the product by consumers?**
- **What are the characteristics of the users?**
- **What technology is required?**
- **What is the current/future competition and what are their products?**
- **Who is the market leader?**
- **How did competitors start?**
- **What markets are they in and what are their plans?**

Without the adoption of a strategic assessment of such issues, the control and monitoring of strategic objectives may have to take place outside the financial management system using disaggregated measures, thereby losing the ability to consider easily the overall impact of the enterprise's achievements in these areas.

Goldstar Electronics provides an example of these difficulties. It sets its strategic objectives in terms of ability to provide what customers may want – good after-sales service, product development and innovative production management – but does not appraise the achievement of these goals directly using its financial management system. The company relies on a number of familiar indices such as indices of sales growth and of new market development, per capita sales ratios and product mix ratios. These measures, which are not all fully reflective of the chosen goals, may give conflicting signals, may not fully reflect cost factors and cannot be aggregated in a meaningful way.

The use of these and of other non-financial measures related directly to key success factors is in some companies growing and is thought to contribute positively to business activities, not least at the level of the workplace. There is a sharing of information on key success factors and a reporting of these in a way that is more meaningful and particularly more familiar at the higher levels of decision-making.

Adopting a strategic perspective emphasises that each of the firm's strategies for products and markets should yield the customer some benefit. There are two usual strategies: diversification and product enhancement. Each component element of these strategies yields customers possible benefits. (For a detailed discussion see Bromwich 1991). For example, an expanded product portfolio provides the consumer with more choice, and the enhancement of an existing product to improve its quality yields the customer clear benefit if this improvement of product quality is relative to competing firms.

One key perspective that allows strategic management accounting to be deployed is to see each product not as a whole or as a unit but to perceive it as comprising a number of separate characteristics offered to the customer. It is these attributes that actually constitute commodities and that appeal to consumers. Demands for goods are derived from the demands for their underlying characteristics. These attributes might include a variety of quality elements, such as operating performance variables, reliability and warranty arrangements; physical features and service factors, like the assurance of supply and of after-sales service. It is these elements which differentiate products and appeal to consumers. A firm's market share depends on the match between the attributes provided by its products and consumers' tastes and on the supply of these attributes by competitors.

Bromwich (1991) sees strategic management accounting as going beyond collecting data on businesses and their competitors, to consider the benefits that products offer to customers, and how these benefits contribute to building and sustaining competitive advantage. The benefits provided by the product are the ultimate cost drivers. Simply attributing cost to products rather than to benefits overlooks the notions that it is in the market that competitive advantage is achieved, and that commercial success depends upon having a product in demand. The only products that will survive in the market are those that yield the maximum amount of a specific bundle of characteristics for the amount of money the customer wishes to spend. Deciding to provide a product with a particular configuration also requires achieving this at a competitive cost level, which links in with the idea of managing the value-added process in producing any product. An objective of strategic management accounting, is to determine the cost of providing product characteristics to consumers given existing operating condition.

Guilding et al (2000) consider SMA practices as highlighting an external or future focus. They identify fifteen specific techniques: activity based costing, attribute costing, benchmarking, brand valuation budgeting and monitoring, competitor cost assessment, competitive position monitoring, competitor performance appraisal, integrated performance measurement, quality costing, strategic costing, strategic pricing, value chain costing, life cycle costing and target costing. The last two are considered in the next section of the book. Others have been referred to in this and prior sections. It remains clear that any organization appealing to SMA concepts in its accounting practices does so in a highly context specific manner which will not necessarily deploy the above terminology or approaches.

A key question in practice is how active a role financial management executives play in strategic planning activities. In the UK there may have been a manufacturing focus that conditions financial managers to look at internal operational issues rather than outward competitive and market-based factors (Roslender and Hart, 2003). But this is rapidly changing in the global business climate. Where the finance functions must add to the bottom line if it is to be valued. The strategic evaluation of organizational issues might be considered to entail the analysis of a range of diverse factors. Many factors may be relevant in the provision of strategically-oriented management information. These include financial and non-financial information, competitor activities, product characteristics, market share data and other value chain-related information.

There is evidence that SMA can be useful in providing different types of information to assist decision-makers in dealing with a variety of strategic issues. The five most important factors seem to be:

- **competitive pressure;**
- **cost reduction;**
- **productivity improvement;**
- **volume/market share changes;**
- **quality improvement.**

Market environment, competitors' activities, and customer satisfaction are most often regarded as useful factors in strategy formulation. Also competitor activities, market share/market analysis, and financial/non-financial information are most widely used. The information is in part encompassed in the balanced scorecard approach.

Strategic Cost Analysis: Tying Value to Costs

The aim of strategic cost analysis is to determine the costs of providing product characteristics to the consumer, given an existing base of knowledge in cost determination. Many firms, when faced with competitive challenges, undertake comparative investigations of product benefits offered by themselves and their competitors. Often the costs of providing such benefits are not considered in this process and these costs are subjected to the same general cuts as other costs even though increasing them may be required to meet the competitive challenge. Similarly, in automotive firms, product planners developing a new model are often provided with figures based on product characteristics. Such reports can be provided regularly both for planned and existing products. Many of the cost figures needed can be obtained from a re-analysis of existing databases and more detailed analyses of existing figures. Typically, this does not require the existing method of reporting the cost structure of the enterprise to be abandoned. The aim of this type of strategic cost analysis is to attribute some of those costs which are normally treated as product costs to the benefits they provide to the consumer, where these benefits are believed to be of strategic importance.

Not all costs can necessarily be attributed to consumer benefits, and for some costs and benefits such an attribution may not be worth the cost of undertaking the exercise. The first step in a strategic cost analysis of this type is to list separately the product benefits offered to consumers. These benefits will differ fundamentally depending on whether the customer is in the final goods market or is an intermediate firm in the chain leading to the final customer. With the latter type, strategic cost analysis may be useful in facilitating analysis by customer rather than product.

Consider an exercise which attempts to model a fast-food supplier which supplies prepared and partly processed products to its network of selling outlets (see Table 6.3). An illustrative set of consumer benefits are shown on the left axis of the figure. It is assumed that all the firm's products provided similar consumer benefits. These benefits can be categorised in a number of ways. In the figure, those items directly related to a unit of product (items 1-7) are shown separately from those relating to sales outlets (items 8-11). Product advertising provides an example of other benefits not related directly to the other two categories but which can be attributed to the product. The total of costs which can be treated in this way are shown in the row labelled 'total costs attributable to consumer benefits'. The penultimate row is for those product costs that cannot be attributed to consumer benefits. It is included so that the analysis can be reconciled with product costs prepared in the conventional way.

The number of consumer benefits to which it is sought to assign a cost will depend on the strategy adopted by the enterprise. Thus a firm which concentrates on giving high benefits for only a few characteristics will report only the costs associated with these characteristics.

The second step in strategic cost analysis is to decide on a set of cost categories for the product. A variant of the firm's usual cost classification will often be best as this will encompass the matters of concern to that firm and thus reflect its economic environment. In Table 6.3 the overall cost categories chosen are variable product costs, activity-related costs, capacity-related costs and decision-related costs. These costs can be further subdivided into such categories as those given in the note to the figure.

The first cost category shown in Table 6.3 is variable product cost, which shows the normal direct cost of production. The second category is that of the activity- or transaction-related costs attributable to the product. The inclusion of such activity-related costs indicates that the approach is sufficiently flexible to incorporate the results of a variety of ways of collecting costs. Common cost problems arise with strategic cost analysis because costs such as materials, labour and variable overheads may contribute simultaneously to a number of consumer benefits and it may be impossible to attribute part of these costs to each of the consumer benefits to which they contribute. Consider the example of a confectionery business where an operation which blends two or more raw materials together may contribute to a number of consumer benefits, such as appearance, taste and texture. Any assignment of the costs of the operation to these consumer benefits would be arbitrary.

One approach to this problem is to bundle these benefits together for this cost category. For example, a fast-food supplier which sought to be seen as a lower-cost provider of its products using minimally sized and equipped outlets might well only cost the relative value of its products and the costs of providing a good geographical coverage in convenient locations. A more up-market supplier would report on more product and outlet benefits.

The next major category of costs is capacity-related costs, which includes depreciation and land and building occupancy costs. These two cost categories capacity and activity illustrate both advantages and disadvantages of the approach. Their use associates these costs directly with products or groups of products, whereas normally they are aggregated into overheads and allocated on some arbitrary basis. With regard to depreciation and with occupancy costs, as a specific product or class of products is involved, it may be possible in some instances to determine what assets and capacity are attributable to the product or class of product.

Strategic cost analysis, (according to Bromwich 1991 who discusses the issues noted above at length), seeks to report sensibly on the costs of resources that may be important in attracting customers. However, if these costs are just taken from the financial accounting reports, any numbers entered here may have little economic meaning. For many businesses, substituting leasing charges for depreciation charges may be feasible, as may charging a market-based rental for space, especially if these approaches are used in the company's conventional management accounts as they are, for example, by many well known store and hotel chains.

An analysis of this type can be undertaken separately for each group of similar products. There may also be a need for additional statements at the level of the strategic business unit or the enterprise to encompass any number of benefits following from diversification of the enterprise's product portfolio and other benefits generated at this level in the firm, such as non-product-related advertising or conferring a high-tech image for all the firm's products for example.

The final category of costs shown in the diagram, decision-related costs, are those whose level depends not on operational activity but on managerial decisions concerning the level of resources to be provided for certain functions. The costs associated with these decisions will generally not be affected by the actual level of activity in the enterprise at any given time. They are, however, the costs which are often especially geared to providing consumer benefits. Seeking to attribute them to the benefits they are meant to generate represents a way of providing strategically oriented management information since these costs are not rendered visible with conventional accounting where they are subsumed into fixed costs. The approach attempts to focus directly and primarily on costs which are potentially of strategic importance to the enterprise.

Table 6.3 Strategic Cost Analysis: A Fast-Food Supplier

Illustrative costs	Product volume related costs[1]	Activity-related costs[1]	Capacity-related costs[1]	Decision-related costs[1]	Total costs
Product benefits					
1. Textiles					
2. Nutritional value					
3. Appearance					
4. Taste					
5. Consistency of above, over outlets and time					
6. Quality					
7. Low cost relative to competitors					
Outlet benefits					
8. Service					
9. Cleanliness					
10. Outlet facilities					
11. Location and geographical coverage					
Other benefits					
12. Product advertising					
Total costs attributable to consumer benefits					
Product costs not attributable to consumer benefits					
Total product cost					

Source: Bromwich, 1991

Analyzing Customer Profitability

It is now widely recognised that different sources of revenues do not contribute equally to net income. Simply doing business with some customers can reduce a firm's profits and shareholder value. Many instances exist of firms which initially believe all their customers to be profitable. But closer analysis often reveals that many are deeply unprofitable. Managers are frequently not aware that their customer strategy determines customer profitability. That is, customer acquisition, maintenance and development affect profits and ultimately share price.

For many companies, 20 percent of customers generate most of the potential profits, 60 percent contribute little or nothing and the remaining 20 percent actually eat into profits. Figure 6.2 illustrates the situation:

Figure 6.2 The 80:20 Rule

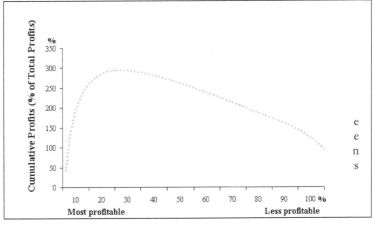

Consider Fidelity Investments – the largest mutual fund company in the world. Fidelity found that some of its customers who drew heavily on channels through which the company interests were actually unprofitable. Fidelity set up automated telephone lines and redesigned its website. The telephone system identified low business customers and routed their calls to longer queues so as to serve the most profitable customers more quickly. Fidelity lost about 4 percent of unprofitable customers. Many low business customers switched to using the web and actually became more satisfied. Ultimately, unprofitable customers became profitable and profitable customers got better service through shorter wait times when calling.

Many management information systems focus not on the customer but on products, departments or geographic regions. Customer accounting profitability (CAP) analysis can provide profitability information on individual customers. At a more aggregate level, it can focus on groupings of customers (e.g., groupings by revenues, size of average transaction, number of transactions or time since the business association began). CAP can also provide information on the profitability of different distribution channels. Within a computer or food company, for example, a CAP analysis might consider major computer chain customers, large retail stores, independent retail stores, corporate accounts and direct-mail accounts.

Revenue differences across customers of a company can arise from many sources, including differences in the:
- prices charged per unit to different customers;
- selling volume levels across customers;
- products or services delivered to different customers;
- items provided without charge to different customers.

Differences in cost across the spectrum of a company's customers arise from differences in the way different customers use the company's resources. Several features of CAP analysis are highly relevant::
- Entire value chain: CAP analysis cuts across costs from potentially all parts of the value chain.
- **Multiple transactions: CAP analysis focuses on multiple transactions of a customer rather than any single transaction.**
- **Multiple products: CAP analysis focuses on multiple products bought by a single customer rather than a single product bought by multiple customers.**
- **Customer-specific costs: CAP analysis captures costs that are related to a customer but are not specific to a product, service, department or geographic area.**
- **Aggregate or narrow focus: CAP analysis can be kept at a highly aggregate level (e.g., different distribution outlets) or**

brought to the very granular level of individual customers.

These features may suggest that changes in the way most management information systems are designed and operated could be required.

Costs can vary depending on how customers draw upon a company's resources such as marketing, distribution, and customer service. If a comprehensive analysis of the benefits and costs of customer relationships is not undertaken, companies can unknowingly continue to service unprofitable customers. It is therefore important to carry out thorough analyses of the costs and benefits of customers before deciding which customers to service and how to strategically price the firm's products and services.

The management accountancy association CMA Canada which trains strategic financial management professionals has issued a guideline which makes it clear that many costs are often hidden within the production, support, marketing, and general administrative areas. Hidden customer costs may include items such as the following:

- stock carrying costs;
- stocking and handling costs;
- quality control and inspection costs;
- customer order processing;
- order picking and order fulfilment;
- billing, collection and payment processing costs;
- accounts receivable and carrying costs;
- customer service costs;
- wholesale service and quality assurance costs.
- selling and marketing costs.

Naturally, different sources of revenue have different profitability implications. This applies to all customers, new and established. Customer profitability measures can reveal that some newly acquired customers are unprofitable as a result of high customer acquisition costs. In early periods, this cost may not be covered by the margins earned through selling products and services to the customers. In these cases, lifetime profitability analysis and product life cycle costing can help in assessing the basis for retaining these customers. In many instances, customers that are unprofitable in the short-run may become very profitable as their purchases increase and their cost to service decreases. Likewise, customers that are unprofitable in the long-term may require immediate action to turn them towards profitability. This may include promoting more cross-selling opportunities to enhance the product range of customer purchases. Moreover, other customers may be prestigious to retain, even when they are unprofitable on their own account; as long as they contribute to the perception of reputation and credibility of the company, and improve the ability to sell to others, they may add to the company's profitability.

Customer profitability analysis can draw significantly on an organization's resources. Barriers to implementation can include:
- convincing management that potential organizational improvements justify the resource allocation;
- obtaining the significant required resources that include information technology, equipment, and staff for analysis and preparation;
- changing the sales incentive system to reward customer profitability rather than sales volume;
- obtaining buy-in from employees within the company who are often reluctant to change;
- training employees in the use of customer profitability analysis and its measurement and rewards.

Strategy and Customer Profitability Analysis

Many organizations have a fairly wide range of products and customers and, knowing the profit contribution of each one, while important in itself, is insufficient in helping to frame or modify commercial policies or strategy. To achieve this, and to focus management attention on action, it is important to be able to analyse such data. Cumulative customer contribution analysis can be helpful, whether applied to product or customer profitability analysis, by making patterns visible in the way that numbers alone do not (see Develin and Bellis-Jones, 1999, for an extended discussion).

According to these authors, cumulative customer contribution analysis (CCCA) highlights how major resources (and assets) frequently stand behind those customers that generate only marginal or negative contributions. It attempts to illustrate graphically the extent of profit erosion by customers with servicing costs that exceed the margins which they generate See Figure 6.3).

Figure 6.3 Cumulative customer profitability analysis

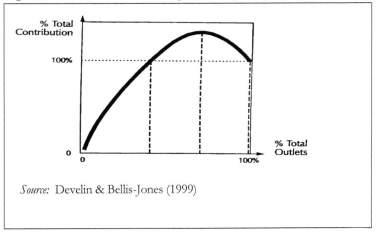

Source: Develin & Bellis-Jones (1999)

Graphs such as those shown in Figures 6.2 and 6.3 reveal examples of profit erosion to the extent of 20 to 60 per cent of the profit which has already been generated. Develin and Bellis-Jones (1999) suggest that a decision grid analysis (DGA) can be useful in providing a perspective on customers vis-à-vis strategy. The DGA plots each customer account on a graph of profitability against volumes of business, as illustrated in Figure 6.4.

Figure 6.4 Decision Grid Analysis

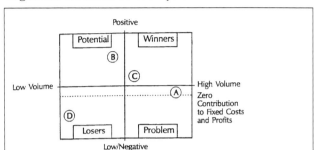

Source: Develin & Bellis-Jones (1999)

It highlights all customer accounts against one of four categories, each of which may require a different commercial response. It is also the first step in defining the characteristics of a profitable or unprofitable customer, so providing the company with a greater ability to identify, and then focus resources on developing and defending genuinely attractive accounts.

The emphasis on adopting a 'customer focus' has become pervasive across many areas of management. As a result, customer profitability has become central to advances in several high-profile areas of management thinking, including:

- **supporting strategic decisions;**
- **valuing intangible assets;**
- **analysing customer retention rates.**

Supporting strategic decisions: customer profitability systems typically assume that the existing business infrastructure will stay relatively constant in the face of various management decisions. Evidently, the adoption of flexible organizational technologies will alter the contribution made by individual customers where resource input and output relationships are affected.

Valuing intangible assets: most management information systems restrict their attention to the valuation of tangible assets (e.g., property, plant, and equipment; computers; and motor vehicles). In many businesses, however, intangible assets (such as brands the company owns) are a significant component of the company's total value. Brand names are pivotal to valuations of consumer products for companies such as Nokia or Samsung. Similarly, a company's customer base is often a valuable intangible asset. Examples include a doctor's patient base as well as Expedia's or Vodafone's subscriber base. Consequently, valuations of companies for acquisition decisions often recognise customer bases as the single most important asset. Given the importance of customer bases, assessments of management performance should track how the value of customer bases change periodically.

Management decisions can dramatically increase or decrease the value of these intangible assets. For example, consider the effect of implementing a total quality management (TQM) programme for a consumer product that has had a low quality ranking for years. If the TQM programme causes the company's product to be ranked first in quality, this improvement is likely to have both short-run and long-run effects. Financial information systems may, however, only recognise the short-run increase in profit.

One reason for tracking changes in the value of customer bases is to attempt to highlight management actions that focus on the short run. For example, price cuts may well boost short-run profitability for certain key customers, but they may also decrease long-term profitability because customers may begin to expect continued price reductions in the future. The argument for monitoring changes in customer bases is similar to the argument for monitoring changes in brand values.

Models of customer value are in their infancy. Some models take a net present value approach. More refined models would recognise uncertainty in the form of likely competitor responses, differences in customer renewal profiles and alternative ways to compute customer profitability. A separate financial statement focused only on intangible assets may increase their usefulness.

Customer profitability databases could facilitate development of more informed decision-making tools in the following ways:
- **by tracking the resources required to attract new customers and retain existing customers;**
- **by providing more reliable estimates of the operating income derived from new and existing customers.**

Alternative approaches to customer retention such as via lower prices or better customer service may yield different customer retention rates. Refinements in tracking customer profitability may permit more extensive testing of the economics of these alternative approaches.

Managerial decision making which has strategic consequences cannot adopt a narrow technical viewpoint. This section has brought to light many concerns, some operational and others with a wider management purview. Such issues need careful weighing as financial management concern go beyond cost identification – they seek ultimately to transform costs in the light of managerial objectives. Where such transformation has strategic intent, the organization's core activities and pursuits are likely to be reshaped. The decision to deploy strategic finance approaches are essentially managerial rather simply financial.

7

TIMING, MARKET AND STRATEGIC ISSUES

IN 1997, *Kellogg's* Nutri-Grain *was launched originally designed to meet the needs of busy people who had missed breakfast. It aimed to provide a healthy cereal breakfast in a portable and convenient format. It was immediately successful, gaining almost 50% share of the growing cereal bar market in just two years.* Nutri-Grain's *sales steadily increased as the product was promoted and became well known. It maintained growth in sales until 2002. By mid-2004 however, Nutri-Grain found its sales declining whilst the market continued to grow at a rate of 15%. At this point, Kellogg's had to make a key business decision. Sales were falling, the product was in decline and losing its position. Should it be deleted as it was at the end of its product life cycle? After some analysis, Kellogg's decided to extend the product-life cycle of* Nutri-Grain. It repositioned *the brand as healthy and tasty, promoted a new and clearer brand image, placed better offers and materials to stores that sold the product and revised the pricing. Under the label* Soft Bake Bar, *sales went from a decline to substantial growth, with* Elevenses *sales increasing by almost 50%. The* Nutri-Grain *brand achieved a retail sales growth rate of almost three times that of the market and continued growth was maintained after the initial re-launch (http://businesscasestudies.co.uk/kelloggs/extending-the-product-life-cycle). Understanding the financial implications of life-cycle analysis can give enterprises insight on routes to value creation.*

Time and Product Life Cycles

Time and external market issues concern all managers in modern enterprises. At one level, the passage of time has been closely associated with the incursion of costs and the utilization of resources. All organizations confront costs which recur at different periods of time. The categorization of costs as fixed or variable is an inherent reflection of this. A resource such as electric power or water usage is typically considered as having a close relationship with usage over time. Other costs remain fixed over specified time periods. Ultimately, over extended time frames, all costs can be regarded as variable. But time also has another dimension of significance which relates to the life cycle of products. This is explored below.

Over the past two decades, the pace of product development by enterprises has accelerated. Concurrently the time window available for a firm to produce, sell, recuperate costs incurred and attain profitability has shortened given the on-going speed-up of competitive forces. This has altered the perceived need for managerial information and the level of financial analysis detail sought. Managers operating in high-technology companies with rapid product development strategies need to adapt quickly to an ever-changing environment. Many managers are reorienting their focus from cost control to a finance-time orientation as dictated by strategic and market concerns. They are becoming involved in new product development and in carefully orchestrating the use of different financial management issues of strategic relevance. Time concerns have become key to the management of modern enterprises particularly those which have implemented e-business processes. Whilst time is essential to account for in internal financial management, so are customer and market concerns important to strategic management. Configuring both internal productive activities and finance practices to achieve alignment with market factors can be a demanding but necessary expertise for many enterprises. Aside from discussing life cycle issues, this section also considers target-costing practices which more specifically connect market based intelligence to requisite financial management pursuits.

Lifecycle considerations are now important across a large number of industries as new products are developed and replaced increasingly rapidly. It is no longer the case that once developed, a product can maintain acceptability from the consumers' perspective over a long time period. Producers survey markets for potential improvements in exchange for potential profits and consumers screen products to identify state-of-the-art features in the right mix at the right price. High-technology companies, which traditionally have extensive research and development and product development functions, face an environment characterised by rapid technological change, shortened product life cycles and global competition. In such an environment, the ability to develop products rapidly and bring them to market can become a primary source of competitive advantage. Financial control is an ever present issue - not just during production but prior to product launch also.

Product lifecycle begins with the initial product specification and ends with the withdrawal of the product from the marketplace. The production-related stages include product conception and design, product process and development, and production and logistics. Figure 7.1 offers a graphical outline of the stages at which funds are committed for a particular product and the actual cash outflows entailed. A very large portion of the funds committed coincides with product conception and affect actual expenditures following the start of production.

Figure 7.1 Product Life-Cycle: Financial Commitment vs. Cash Outflows

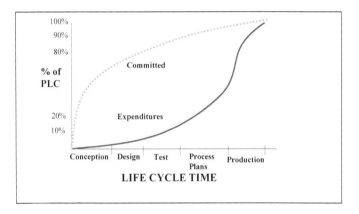

Figure 7.2 is a perspective from the producer's point of view. The curves depict the flow of cash throughout the lifecycle. Starting out in the negative, the bottom curve tracks cumulative cash flows. Once it crosses the horizontal axis, positive cash flows accrue. In managing cash flows, timing becomes crucial, and a costing system closely associated with that timing is important in order to make reasonable decisions about products, particularly those of the go/no-go kind. Figure 7.3 shows a sequence of decisions made throughout the lifecycle alongside the cost impact.

Figure 7.2 Life-Cycle Cost: The Producer's Perspective

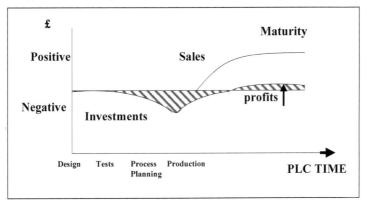

Suppose that a designer is assessing the general configuration of a cellular phone. Should it have a touch screen display? A pull-out ear piece? Built-in MP3? The manufacturing processes that are selected will have some future impact in terms of materials management and financial cost incursions. The choice of the manufacturing process adopted can have significant consequences in relation to materials managements and operational activities. The early decisions are crucial to that whole process. Each time decisions are made at a particular stage of the process, financial analyses are required. In fact, the outcomes of those decisions will become cost drivers throughout the later stages, just as the outcomes of earlier decisions collectively become cost drivers of the present stage. Figure 7.4 shows the various stages with major activities in the lifecycle. Across the top are various characteristics which are to be linked to the stages identified.

Earlier decisions in terms of both materials and other technologies have a potentially significant impact on the eventual producibility of the product. If one looks at a whole series of decisions – R&D, design features, manufacturing technology – all are going to affect product manageability up to the production stage. At each stage, executives make decisions. The decisions, in turn, become drivers of performance downstream in terms of the other activities in the lifecycle. The decisions made at that stage collectively determine the outcomes and cost at subsequent stages.

Product costs may be common to a number of products at the pre-production stages. Many such joint costs cannot be traced to a particular product, especially where one generation of products gives rise to another. Yet, costs incurred often end up being attributed to the first product emerging from the pre-production stages and this possibly reduces the perceived profit potential of that product. This may even dampen the perceived long-term viability of the product and affect related management decisions.

Figure 7.3 Cost Impact Versus Decision

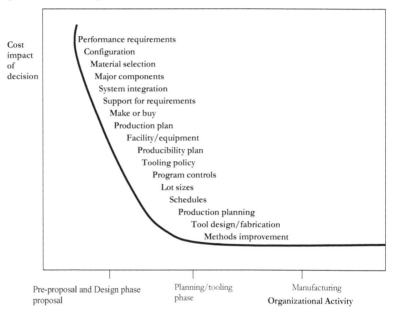

As noted above, it is often the case that most production costs are committed *before* a product is ever produced. It is not uncommon for around 70 per cent of the lifecycle costs of many high-technology products to be determined by the end of the concept stage. As Figure 7.5 shows, the opportunities to realise savings in lifecycle costs diminish rapidly after the concept stage. This is important to recognise as once the product is launched, the contribution margin decreases as market competition becomes more intense (see Figure 7.6).

Figure 7.4 Life-Cycle Costing Decision Relationships

Attributes / Stages	Designability	Producibility	Manageability	Distributability	Saleability	Servicability
R & D	Decisions	- - - - - -	- - - - - -	- - - - - -	- - - - - -	- - - - ▶
Design	◀ Info. -	Decisions	- - - - - -	- - - - - -	- - - - - -	- - - - ▶
Mfg. Eng.	◀ - - - - -	Info. - - -	Decisions	- - - - - -	- - - - - -	- - - - ▶
Pdt. Planning	◀ - - - - -	- - - - - -	Info. - - -	Decisions	- - - - - -	- - - - ▶
Distribution	◀ - - - - -	- - - - - -	- - - - - -	Info. - - -	Decisions	- - - - ▶
Saleability	◀ - - - - -	- - - - - -	- - - - - -	- - - - - -	Info. - - -	Decisions
Field service	◀ - - - - -	- - - - - -	- - - - - -	- - - - - -	Info. - -	Decisions

Source: Adapted from Burnstein, 1988

Systems that can evaluate product costs before manufacturing begins can prove useful in enabling higher levels of competitiveness through better management information. To that end, many companies have reformed their cost management efforts upstream from manufacturing to the product development process.

Figure 7.5 Targeting Savings

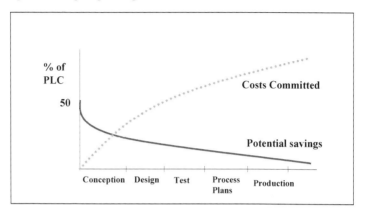

Figure 7.6 Contribution per Unit vs. Phase of Product Life Cycle

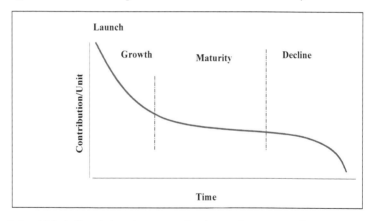

It is widely believed that time to market is a major source of competitive advantage. The primary advantage of accelerated product development is that an innovator or "prospector" can charge premium prices in the early years of a product's life cycle. Process improvement initiatives can then be effected to realise savings in later years. Late entrants may have to go to extraordinary lengths to succeed. Some internet players have witnessed a first mover advantage whereby 'eyeball' volume, site stickiness and brand names are established much faster by the first entrants in different sectors, both in business-to-consumer and business-to-business contexts. Naturally, high site traffic does not necessarily materialise into profits. Other web-based companies have succeeded in surpassing the performance of "first movers" by learning from market incumbents' experiences and altering their management strategies accordingly. Like cost management systems, life cycles tend to be industry and even enterprise specific.

Strategy and Target Cost Management

Strategy may be considered to guide organizational initiatives. With intense competition for global markets and decreasing product lifecycles, companies often assess carefully the competitive forces that affect each line of business. This can be done using Porter's (1985, 1998) model in terms of competitors, new entrants, substitution possibilities, bargaining power of buyers and bargaining power of suppliers.

For high-technology companies, the threat from competitors and the threat of substitution can create tremendous pressures to develop new products and rapidly bring them to market. Core competencies can be leveraged to rapidly develop new products in several different lines of business. For a growing range of products, the development stage can entail a variety of decisions which culminate in major future resource commitments. These decisions can factor in cost reduction options which will be of benefit once production begins. Target costing can play a significant role prior to the start of production.

Target cost management is aimed at supporting the cost reduction process at the development and design stages of a new product or for a model modification. This contrasts with <u>kaizen costing</u> which attempts to support cost reduction in the manufacturing phase of an existing model of product. Kaizen refers to the continuous accumulation of small improvements rather than innovative product enhancement.
Target cost management (or targets costing for short) comprises two processes classified as (1) the process of planning a specific product that

satisfies customers' needs and of establishing the target cost from the target profit and targeted sales price of the new product, and (2) the process of realising the target cost by using value engineering (VE) and a comparison of target costs with achieved costs. The basic idea of VE is that products and services have functions to perform and the amount of their value is measured by the ratio of these functions to their costs. By this process, the decision as to whether the product is to be produced is made. For this purpose, it is necessary that the functions of each product, part and service are clarified and that all functions are subject to quantification of a type which enables their significance, cost effectiveness and customer perception to be approximated.

In general, target costing has the following properties
- **It is applied at the development and design stage and differs from 'kaizen' cost control which is applied in the production stage.**
- **It stresses cost reduction rather than tracing.**
- **The target costing process, company-based management expertise and production engineering methods can be useful if integrated.**
- **Co-operation between departments and their interaction is essential to the execution of target costing.**
- **It is more suitable in the multi-product, small production run firm than in the few-products, large production run firm.**

Kato, Böer and Chow (1995) consider target costing to be much more than a simple technique of setting cost targets: They see it as an integrative mechanism to link the various functional areas of a business into a coherent system. In companies that have used target costing successfully, information flows smoothly among marketing researchers, product designers, manufacturing personnel, and cost analysts. The target costing process is closely tied to the strategic planning process because target costing encompasses a broad range of both upstream and downstream costs from manufacturing. Target costing is a tool that is:
is future oriented;
- **focuses designers' attention on the cost implications of design decisions;**
- **helps managers evaluate the profitability of a product before it is produced.**

Of essence is the determination of target cost as the outcome rather than the starting premise for operational activities.

Target costing requires managers and engineers to constantly estimate the production cost of a product as it moves through the design process. Information from all parts of the organization is likely to be required. Instead of being a passive and isolated part of the management process, target costing is shapes enterprises actively transcending the narrow boundaries of enterprise functional areas.

Putting Target Costing Principles into Effect

Although organizations differ in their approaches to target cost management, some basic elements relate to target costing. These can be identified as follows:

Long- and medium-term profit plans for the whole company are established and the overall target profit for each period is determined for each product. In computing operating profits, depreciation costs of facilities, development costs and prototype manufacturing costs are allocated to each model. The ratio of return on sales is often used as the indicator of the profit ratio for establishing target profit because this ratio is easily computed for each product.

Subsequently, in order to give shape to the general new product plan, details of the type of new product to be developed and the content of the model changes based on market research are determined. The basic plan for a specific new product is then identified. In this step, the major cost factors such as design and structure are determined and target costs are established. Each department needs to review the material requirements and the manufacturing process, and to estimate costs. According to the reports of the departments, the total 'estimated cost' is computed.

At the same time, target price figures are gathered from company sources. From these prices and target profit, an <u>allowable cost</u> is computed. The computation is as follows:
target sales price − target profit = allowable cost

Allowable cost is the cost that is sought to be achieved, but it is necessary to establish a 'target cost' that is attainable and which motivates employees to make efforts to ultimately reach the 'allowable cost'. The establishment of the target cost needs to be reviewed along various dimensions regarding the size of the gap between allowable cost and estimated cost. After the target cost is determined, the departments co-operate in implementing VE activities regarding the design method in order to identify cost-effective products that will fulfil customers' demands.

The target cost is decomposed into cost elements and functional elements. <u>Cost elements</u> are typically material costs, purchased parts costs, direct labour costs, depreciation costs and so on. For a motorcar, for instance, functional elements include engine, transmission system and chassis. Important points are clarified by these detailed classifications. An example of a form for classification is shown in Figure 7.7.

<u>Functional analysis</u> is carried out to learn more about the cost of providing functions vis-à-vis their volume. The technique mainly involves the following basic VE steps including
Choosing the object of analysis, such as product, service or overhead area.
Selecting members of a team.
Defining the functions of the object.
Evaluating the functions.
Suggesting alternatives and compare these with the target cost.
Choosing the alternatives for manufacturing.
Reviewing the actual results.

Figure 7.7 Form for Classification of Target Costs : Motorcar

Cost elements \ Functions	Material cost £	Purchased Parts costs £	Direct labour costs £	.....	Total £
Engine					
Transmission System					
Chassis					
.					
.					
.					
.					
.					
Total					

At the product design stage a trial blueprint can be drafted according to the target cost set for every part. Information from each department is required at this stage. If there is a gap between the target cost and the estimated cost, the departments undertake VE analysis and the trial blueprint is adjusted accordingly. After repeating this process several times, a final blueprint is established.

In the production planning step, the necessary production equipment is obtained to match costs according to the final blueprint. Standard values of material consumption, labour hours and so on are established. Once the target cost is set, production begins. Performance evaluation of target costing is then implemented.

The performance evaluation of target costing is implemented to examine the degree to which the target cost is achieved. If the target cost is not achieved, investigations are made to clarify where the responsibility lies and where the gap arises. These investigations also evaluate the effectiveness of the target costing activities. Once production is under way, kaizen costing can begin. Kaizen costing activities include cost reduction activities which require changes in the way the company manufactures existing products.

Kaizen costing activities are of two kinds. One consists of activities implemented to enhance actual performance when the difference between actual cost and target cost is large. This entails implementing activities periodically to reduce any differences between target and estimated profit and to achieve 'allowable cost'.

The second category of kaizen costing aids in reaching cost reduction targets established for every department as a result of the short-term profit plan. Thus, for example, the variable costs such as direct materials, energy and direct labour costs are managed by setting the amount of kaizen cost per unit of each product type.

Two major changes in operating environments have led managers to recognise that cost considerations should be addressed earlier in the product life cycle, according to Fisher (1995). First, automation has changed the cost structure of many companies, so more costs are fixed in the short run. This change in cost mix has caused less emphasis on typical management accounting tools such as cost-volume-profit analysis and break-even analysis. Given a high level of automation, most production costs are determined in the product planning and design stages, so reducing product costs dramatically in the production stage is difficult, if not impossible. Most of the life cycle of a product is determined by the time the design stage is completed.

Second, shortening of the product life cycle has increased the importance of delivering a competitive product to the market quickly. Any errors in product cost or product quality are difficult to correct quickly because product life cycles are so short.

Historically, most cost reduction and cost control efforts have focused on the production stage of the product life cycle. Budgeting and standard cost systems are prime examples of this type of cost control. The chief concern at the product planning and design stages has been product performance and product scheduling, with little attention to product cost. Unfortunately, almost all production capabilities and costs are set during production planning and design; they are fixed once production begins.

The lack of concern about product cost in the product planning and design stages may cause reduced profitability. Because of changes in the business environment, many companies now recognise the importance of cost reduction efforts early in the product life cycle. Opportunities for cost reduction early in the product life cycle (i.e., during the planning and design stages) exceed those later in the life cycle (production). Target costing may be considered to be a logical systematic process for reducing product costs in the product planning stage since this is where the greatest cost reduction possibilities lie.

Strategic Synergy in Action

As noted above, target cost management is crucial where market, timing and cost concerns are paramount. Cross-functional communication among management is essential. Increasingly, enterprises creating complex products are facing the challenge of creating synergistic environments. In such firms, breaking down cross functional boundaries becomes essential. Motor car manufacturers are increasingly moving toward establishing platforms for interactions between managers from different specialties and between organizational units to achieve competitiveness and profitable products. GM, Fiat and Porsche provide excellent examples of strategically mobilising synergies.

Welch (*Business Week*, 18/6/07, p72) notes that in the motor car industry more models are jockeying for drivers' attention than ever before. Most cars have acceptable if not excellent quality these days, so finding a way to differentiation becomes all the more important. He explains: In the past, designing a GM vehicle went something like this: The engineers, marketers, and finance folks would devise a long list of specifications – everything from how much headroom the car would have to which materials would cut costs. Then they would present the list to the designers. Today at GM, design comes up with the vision. Then engineering and marketing have an input, making their case perhaps for more interior space, more fuel-efficient aerodynamics, or body changes that might be cheaper to manufacture. Compromises are hammered out in regular meetings.

Understanding that the designers and engineers needed to "start feeling each other's pain", GM has begun holding design workshops. Welch explains that at one meeting the designers explained why pushing the wheels to the corners, for example, communicates strength and athleticism much the same way that pillars at each corner of a building telegraph stability. They suggested that a long, sweeping hood sparks desire among consumers.

The engineers taught the designers about what still needs to happen for cars to achieve decent safety ratings. They explained why a concept car that looks cool on paper would be problematic to engineer. When designer Clay Dean sat down with his team to brainstorm the new Chevrolet Malibu , he knew he needed to find an inexpensive way to transcend its cheap prices. To get there, his team looked at low-price consumer brands that use a dash of design flair to impart cachet. Dean employed a few design tricks: he wrapped the headlights around the edge of the car to make the front wheels look closer to the front than they really are and lends the Malibu classic proportions that people seem drawn to. Actually pushing the wheels farther forward would have cost millions in development and production costs. The interactions between designers, engineers and marketers is positively espoused today at GM as a break from the past.

Now consider Fiat. Faris (*Fortune*, 14/5/07, p33) describes how in 2004 Fiat was going to lose more than $1 billion. Its share of the Italian market had slipped from 52% at the beginning of the 1990s to below 28%. Investments were low, and the management culture was stagnant. Its CEO Marchionne, started to strip the company clear and hammer it into shape. Ten percent of the roughly 20,000 white-collar employees in and around Turin were fired. "This was a very hierarchical, status-driven, relationship-driven organization." says Marchionne. "All that got blown up in July 2004." By 2006, revenues reached $31.3 billion, up 35% from 2005. Trading profits, flipped from red to black, from $332 million in losses in 2005 to a $384 million profit. At a time when many of the industry's major players were struggling, Marchionne accomplished the almost impossible. He did so by flushing out the management, lubricating the design process, revving up production, fine-tuning union relations. In early 2007, the company's market capitalization reached $32.5 billion more than that of GM. To cement this success, Fiat will roll out 23 new vehicles and as many model face-lifts by the end of 2010. Its CEO predicts that net profits for the Fiat Group will nearly triple by 2010.

Marchionne drives his executives to take risks: "They have a huge amount of freedom," he says. "But the freedom has a very expensive pricetag: the delivery of results." Ultimately, the new Fiat culture operates by giving executives incentives to interact with each other in ways that drive value rather than leverage personal power or pursuits that do not align with corporate objectives.

Alfa Romeo which is owned by Fiat is an example of the new approach. It is headed by Baravalle in the UK who says that Marchionne's challenge to him was, "Tell me how to be No. 1 - we can no longer have an incremental philosophy. It has to be a policy of breakthroughs." Under the old management, the brand would have targeted its nearest competitors, fine-tuning quality, marketing, and customer care. "If this year we were in 27th place, next year we would try for 22nd". After commissioning a study comparing Alfa Romeo to its highest-ranked competitors, Lexus, Baravalle scrapped 60% of his dealer network overnight. He restructured the spare-parts division and set up a predelivery centre to give cars a last going-over before they reached the dealer. Managerial interaction was key. Alfa Romeo's worldwide sales of the brand recently rose 17%.

The changes at the Mirafiori plant in Turin were similar. Before Marchionne took over, engineering for each brand was run independently. Fiat would commission its own research. Alfa Romeo would design its own components. Lancia would engineer its own cars. None built on what the others had accomplished. Only two of the company's 19 independently developed platforms shared the same heating, ventilation, and air-conditioning systems. Harold Wester Head of Engineering then launched a plant to produce 85% of Fiat Automobiles' cars on just four platforms. Two cars of the same size are to share two-thirds of their components, most of them not visible to the customer: "You cannot survive with small steps," he says. "You need to leapfrog." Such leapfrogging cannot emerge from functional sylos. Synergies have to be strategically extracted from the existing resources.

In 2007, Fiat launched the Bravo, the first car Marchionne has overseen from its conception. It is a culmination of his reforms, share two-thirds of its components with its predecessor, the Stilo, which continues to be offered as a station wagon. Development from the first sketch to production line took 18 months - an industry record. The Bravo boasts sporty, organic curves like the muscled head of a bull. "we got quite inspired by the Italian ladies," says Christopher Reitz, head designer for the Fiat brand. "we started talking about Sophia Loren with the cat's-eye taillights." The recent success of Fiat rides on the creation of organizational synergies and managerial interconnectedness.

The creation of strategic synergism is also part of the recent successes at Porsche and VW. Wiedeking the Porsche CEO was appointed in 1993 at a time Porsche was weak with an output of 15,000 cars a year. Wiedeking used his production expertise and strategic savvy to turn it around. Today Porsche earns more money per car than any other carmaker (a margin of almost one fifth on each sale). Porsche has increased its stake in VW to 30.9% recently. The difference in scale, style, and profitability between the two companies is huge. VW is the fourth-largest auto manufacturer (after Toyota, GM, and Ford). It employs 325,000 workers to make 5.7 million vehicles. Porsche, is now the 34th- biggest auto company with 11,000-plus employees producing over 100,000 vehicles. Where is the synergy in the mouse asking the elephant to the ball? Only about 20% of what makes a Porsche a Porsche – largely the engine and transmission – are made by Porsche workers. The rest is outsourced. To whom?: mainly to VW. The Cayenne SUV, for example, was engineered alongside VW's own SUV, the Touareg. The steel structure for both vehicles is welded together on the same VW assembly line in Slovakia. The Panamera, Porche's first four-door sports car, has a body assembled and painted by VW at a plant in Hanover. Buying a stake in VW protected Porsche's access to VW factories. Porsche's stock has climbed almost 200%. Has VW benefited? VW's stock price has also more than doubled since the growth in Porsche's investment in VW.

Economic value both for Porsche and VW stem from the two companies' abilities to share knowledge, interact and create strategic synergies. Similar arguments can be made for the changes witnessed at GM and at Fiat. The role of strategic finance in both identifying, tracking and enabling the outcomes of such synergies remains. The potential of strategic finance stems from the fact that it does not maintain traditional demarcations between managerial forms of functional expertise.

8

FINANCIAL MANAGEMENT AND DIGITIZATION

Logic is often transitory. Digital technologies have turned what were once crazy ideas into essential products today. Google's CEO Larry Page came up with the idea of scanning every book ever printed to create the world's biggest library; to build a machine that can translate between any two languages; to photograph every centimetre of every street to create a digital replica of the real world. Google's creation of a Lexus SUV that drives itself via high-tech tools including radars, sensors and laser scanners that take 1.5 million measurements per second may lead us to one day think that driverless cars are a 'must-have'. Digitization has been a major creator of enterprise value over the past decade. Finance expertise must keep pace.

Digitization and Disruption

Technology's influence extends beyond just the particular function of products. Sometimes, technological advances have side impacts and unintended consequences of far reaching significance for economic activity. History presents many examples. In the nineteenth century, railroads altered the economics of transportation and transformed what could be produced, how, where and by whom. Railroads in turn changed the retail industry landscape. Department stores in city centres expanded rapidly because railroads enabled consumers to travel into towns from suburbs. The motorcar likewise altered the structure of the workforce particularly from the 1920s and further enhanced consumer mobility. Shopping centres on the outskirts of towns grew as more individuals gained access to motorcar transportation. From about this time, the development of electric lifts allowed the construction of high-rise buildings bringing thousands of individuals closer to one another with attendant consequences on industrial activities, enterprise productivity and economic output.

Certain effects of technological change can significantly affect organizational strategies for growth and the structuring of whole industries. For instance, some technologies impact the economics of output creating network effects. Phones, fax machines and computer operating systems offer inherent value to users. But this value also grows with the number of users deploying the technology. This is because standards that achieve ubiquity expand the potential deployability of the technology to users. There is thus a potential to drive economic growth via the first order effects of the function or service provided by the technology itself. But then, second order effects arise where the population of users of the technology expands because that very population attracts further increases in size.

Digitization is core to what many regard as the "new economy". The term new economy, however, tends to arouse people's emotions – some are passionate about it – others say it does not exist. Whether or not a new economy exists is inconsequential. The same may be said of the term "Web 2.0". To some this simply refers to new technological devices, digital platforms and communicative innovations. Others, regard it as the start of a new paradigmatic shift in values, perceptions and experiences through technology. The idea that we now live in a "flat" world has been described in similar terms. What matters is that notions of a new economy or of Web 2.0 or of a flattened world mobilise change. Those who believe in their existence may act on their beliefs and do things differently. Those who do not, can take action which alters their enterprise in some ways. Ultimately, organizations change, institutions change and management decisions change as a result of beliefs concerning economic newness. When we think about financial management – there is a parallel. Beliefs which lead managers to alter costs, prices, incentive schemes, quality controls, financial monitors, etc., also extensively reorder many other organizational processes.

Connections between the notion of a new economy and financial management practices exist because "newness" translates into the creation of new business models and novel economic architectures for creating corporate value. When an enterprise implements a new strategy based on altered economic reasoning, financial controls will also change. Transformations in accounting and finance are most pronounced when an enterprise pursues innovative business models – it is such innovativeness that has led many to affirm the notion of a new economy. This section draws out some links between new economy thinking and implications for financial management practices.

Given that many business commentators suggest that the new economy is inciting change, it is probably worth considering what these individuals understand by the term. Many new economy commentators suggest that we have undergone a transformation initially from an agricultural economy where land and labour mattered most, to an industrial era where capital and labour mattered most. More recently, yet another transformation has occurred whereby we have entered a new economic age with information and intellectual capital playing a major role. Possibly, the new economy is a term that signals our inability to grapple with the pace of change. For some, it is representative of a need for a new paradigm as the gap between the world and our understanding of it grows wider.

Those who have written about what is different in the new economy point out that it is powered by information technology and is dependent on intelligence organized around computer networks. This implies that organizational innovation is more and more a function not just of highly skilled labour but also of "the existence of knowledge–creating organizations" (Castells, 2001, p.99). Knowledge creation at the enterprise management level lends itself to novel ways of organizing and to new business models.

As noted above, just as the "new economy" became synonymous with epochal change for some, so has the view that we are now experiencing a "flattening of the world" (Friedman, 2005). This will come to be regarded as "one of those fundamental changes – like the rise of the nation–state or the Industrial Revolution – each of which… produced changes in the role of individuals, the role and form of governments, the way we innovated, the way we conducted business, the role of woman, the way we fought wars, the way we educated ourselves, the way religion responded, the way art was expressed, the way science and research were conducted, not to mention the political labels we assigned ourselves and to our opponents".

Friedman (2005. p 47) notes in addition that "there is something about the flattening of the world that is going to be qualitatively different from other such profound changes: the speed and breadth with which it is taking hold…The flattening process is happening at warp speed... The faster and broader this transition to a new era, the more likely is the potential for disruption". Others contest the view that the world is flat. Ghemawat (2013) argues that in the 'World 3.0,' greater openness and transparency results in more extensive technological, cultural, and social benefits. Knowledge transfer via people, trade, and investments can significantly affect growth.

The causes of the flattening of the world to whatever extent it takes place cannot all be regarded as linked to technological change. But most who deploy technology are affected by its use. This includes the rise of free market capitalism, insourcing, outsourcing, offshoring, supply-chaining and a new era of information access among others. The ongoing dislocating technological disruption suggests extensive alterations in enterprise value creation and in financial management practices.

Ultimately, notions of a new economy, Web 2.0 or the flattening of the world are tied to whether newness is sufficiently radical rather than minimally incremental, and demonstrably transformational rather than evolutionary. One needs to ask how distinct something must be from the familiar to be categorized as new and how new it must be to really be new. This is an important question because advocates of change in financial management have in the past tended to voice their exhortations with greater amplitude to match the perceived degree of newness or disruption. For the purposes of this section the discussion recognizes that economic change is prevalent throughout economies, markets and commercial spaces but that its impact takes different and unpredictable forms. The recent fast pace of economic change in many enterprise contexts has differing implications for financial management. This concern guides the discussion that follows concerning enterprise practices arising alongside digitisation and wide economic change.

Levels of Impact

Novel products and new services emerge in the modern economy at a pace which closely matches technological advances. The advent of digitisation has given rise to information goods such as e-books, digital music recordings and mobile messaging platforms among others. Information intensive services such as web-based airline bookings and car-rental reservation systems and internet-based courier tracking facilities are now commonplace. They provide benefits to consumers (or value takers) who guide the activities of firms (value makers) who, in turn, seek to benefit commercially from these innovations. For many industries, digitization embedded within technological offerings and processes underpin the value created and the basis of exchange. Financial and cost management practices, therefore, can be expected to alter so as to align with the types of costs incurred and the revenues generated. There are three dimensions of concern: managerial issues, organisational concerns and wider macro-economic level implications. At a managerial level, firms will seek to analyse strategic issues, pricing approaches, quality factors and an array of other financial factors affecting the enterprise's economic viability and success. Such managerial considerations are discussed below.

Managerial Strategy

Management thinkers have generally tended to consider decision-making and actions to occur sequentially. The age-old notion that some individuals are meant to think whilst others engage in action became a characteristic feature of industrial management at the turn of the last century with the rise of Taylorism. Conceiving ways of doing things is often now seen as a distinct activity from the actual execution of desired activities. This notion is embedded across virtually every prescribed approach to enterprise management including financial management. Financial managers are today exhorted to be more strategic, and given the fervour with which professional management accountancy bodies are embracing a more strategic posture for the field, strategic thinking in the practice of financial management is an increasingly important issue. Writings concerned with strategic aspects of financial management suggest that practitioners "should reposition their role within organizations to have a strategic focus" (Nyamori et al, 2001, p.65). Many financial management approaches, including activity-based management, product life-cycle costing, target cost management, customer profitability analyses and strategic investment appraisal among others, have been predicated on the idea that strategic thinking should guide managerial actions, including those concerning technological investments. In other words, conceptions of intent should be formulated prior to the implementation of decisions.

In the context of operating as a web-enabled enterprise, the notion that strategic decisions should precede technological choices is largely inappropriate. Some commentators have argued that in "the New Economy, strategic decisions ... are co-mingled with technological decisions" (Rayport and Jaworski, 2001, p.5). The claim has been made that "business strategy that ignores how technology is changing markets, competition and processes is a process for the old economy not the new economy" (Earl, 2000, p.6). This means that digital businesses cannot extract technological choices from their strategic decision-making processes. Consider for instance the CEO of Amazon.com who remarks that personalization recommendations to customers is a "key differentiating factor" (Jeff Bezos, cited in *Business 2.0*. August 2007, p. 54). The technology enabling the achievement of this strategy is complex and intricately bound in the product purchase decision. Strategy and technology related decisions are intertwined. The payoff is not insignificant: Forrester Research reports that recommendation systems can account for up to 30% of an online retailer's sales. The meshing of strategic and technological decisions suggests that there is a need to reformulate financial management precepts in at least some contexts whereby reported financial management information intended for strategic decision-making becomes infused with an understanding of technological possibilities and issues.

In the past, an enterprise may have been able to identify a strategy to modernise production processes. Decision-makers would then have been presented with technological improvement investment options. Supporting accounting and financial information on the likely economic implications would subsequently have been collated and supplied to the decision-makers such that managerial action would rest on appropriate financial analyses of possible technological options stemming from the strategy being pursued. The sequence could be structured as follows:

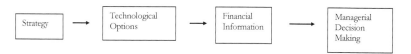

But the co-mingling of strategic and technological decisions within modern organizations implies that managerially useful information can no longer be purely financial and accounting data that treats strategic intent and technological option as distinct elements that are separable from one another and which follow a sequential path. What constitutes relevant information underpinning the economics of organizational activities in a digitised networked world has to be reflective of the realities of the digitized commercial spaces.

Consequently, financial management must increasingly be about the effective representation of strategic and technological interdependencies so as to enable managerial decisions that align with present day organizational realities. This may be depicted as follows:

Thus, in some situations, the marriage of strategy and technology is joined by financial management as a third partner. Consider again Intel. One of the co-founders – Gordon Moore – suggested in the mid-1960's that chipmakers should be able to double the number of transistors and electronic components that can be etched on a chip about every year. When Intel began operations in 1968, Moore's "law" was not articulated as part of the corporate mission intent. But in the early 1980's, this notional function became part of the strategy. Technology was to expand in line with Moore's prediction which in turn led to analyses of its economic consequences:

Intel currently enforces Moore's law which is seen as "a philosophy as well as a strategy" (Sunlin Chou cited in Schlender, 2002, p.41). Intel might now engage in technological investments such that when a state-of-the-art chip plant is opened, the cost of producing a chip falls by literally one-third overnight. Effectively, Intel integrates strategy, technology and financial priorities. Enterprises like Intel consider technology issues to be coupled with strategic and financial considerations. Their interrelationships make it difficult for financial management activities to exist in a vacuum. Financial management decisions-based information is integral to and immanent within assessments of technological, strategic and financial considerations:

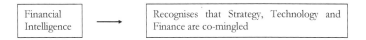

Pricing

Until the 1980's, many financial management commentators stressed the relevance of standard costing systems in the setting of prices. Whole chapters within educational texts in the area were devoted to cost-based pricing. In the late 1980's, the popular management literature began to make much of the desirability for market responsiveness and knowledge about the competition in pricing approaches. Standard costing systems' effectiveness and relevance started to be questioned. The term "benchmarking" entered the management accounting vocabulary. Management gurus like Michael Porter wrote about "competitive strategy" (1988) and the rationale for more intimately understanding market forces. Tom Peters (1985) discussed "corporate excellence" and the need to be more customer orientated. In 1988, Hiromoto described target costing practices within Japanese enterprises in the *Harvard Business Review*. This was followed by the publication of many articles in management journals and magazines about price-led costing. The prescriptive and descriptive literature in cost management, markets and competitive forces is now quite substantial. But there are signs that the deployment of digital technologies by enterprises is changing much of this thinking.

Part of the reason is that internet-based technologies have altered the possibilities of satisfying customer demands and perceptions of viable consumer offerings. Up to the 1970's, consumers were price takers and product takers. The customer was given little say in how the product should be designed or priced. The seller was king. During the 1980's and 1990's, consumers transitioned to becoming price makers and product takers.

Negotiations over price for given products became acceptable in the face of growing numbers of market incumbents competing against each other. Today, with increasing frequency, consumers are price makers and product makers in many industries. Moreover, both price making and product making is taking place at faster speeds – sometimes in real time.

Presently, five per cent of the global economy is engaged in consumer-directed product design. This is likely to continue to expand extensively as interactive, on-line systems that allow individual customers to design their own products by choosing from a menu of attributes, components, prices, and delivery options. The customer's selection sends signals to the supplier's manufacturing system that set in motion the wheel of procurement, assembly, and delivery. Web-enabled choice options can be tied to flexible organizational technologies and computer integrated manufacturing systems making direct access and production triggered by consumers possible. They enable internet driven transformation of consumers from "product takers" to "product makers". Whereas consumers traditionally accepted that the firm carry out the design function, this task is being transferred to the market where viable. For instance, certain on-line music sites allow customers to choose music tracks from different albums and compile their own downloadable personalized albums of prior recordings. Here the customer becomes the product designer as well as consumer with minimal guidance or training.

The transfer of the product design function has implications for the structure of product life-cycles. It raises questions as to what defines the "launch" of a product and how far pre-manufacturing design activities determine the extent of committed production costs and indeed, who and what determines post-production costs and how this alters the control of Kaizen efforts. Inputs into conformance-related quality costs likewise need to be questioned. In broad terms, customers' sophistication in defining product features and price characteristics is growing in many contexts such that supporting financial and cost management systems need to be online and to operate on a real time basis.

Throughout the twentieth century, fixed pricing dominated commercial activities. Possibly this was because the technology was not there for continuous price revisions. As noted, consumers today are, in many instances, price takers and price makers. But, in addition, pricing may be fixed or variable. Variable costing was heavily advocated in the 1960's and 1970's in financial management and accounting books. Activity based costing and target costing became prominent if not replacements in the 1980's and 1990's. Now, given the advances made by digital technologies in reconfiguring organizational activities and the growing sophistication of markets and consumers, we are entering an era of <u>variable pricing</u>. So just as absorption costing gave way to variable costing, and just as fixed costs became delayered by activity-based costing, now is the time to ponder over whether fixed pricing will permanently give way to variable pricing in many product markets. Lawrence (*Information Age*) May 2007, p. 18) notes that: The variable pricing revolution has quietly taken root, aided by a combination of technologies that businesses use to set prices in almost every major market. These technologies include customer profiling and analytics, data warehousing, pricing optimization, revenue management and event processing systems. These technologies are costly and difficult to implement and integrate, but suppliers are able to take much greater control over their pricing – varying prices not just for the benefit of the customer but according to their own objectives. They can price dynamically to respond to demand, to create demand, to reduce waste and to turn over stock more rapidly. In some instances, online retailers regard customer profiling and targeted pricing as a direct response to the impact of online price comparison websites, which threaten to constrain margins. By making special 'one-to-one' and private offers to customers, retailers can keep many of their real prices opaque, invisible to the price crawlers that trawl through their sites and narrow their profits. Prices increasingly vary more and more from customer to customer and across short time periods, for a growing range of products and services. Variable pricing takes many forms of targeted pricing that is having the most impact outside.

Targeted pricing focuses on both groups and on individuals. An example is Avivia's Norwich Union company an insurance group that introduced a pay-as-you drive insurance scheme. Young drivers are charged according to each individual journey, and the risks these journeys pose, rather than being charged one very high annual premium based on a demographic profile. Retailers have also invested in dynamic pricing systems, so they can vary their prices to stimulate demand, turn over stock and maximize margins. Their focus now is mostly on targeted pricing, based on customer analytics. Tesco in the UK provides an example of how pricing can vary: a customer with a Capital One card is classed as a more price sensitive buyer than one with an American Express card. And if they are buying jewellery, for example, they tend to buy aspirationally. Such buyers might be offered discounted branded goods, whereas the Amex card holders would not. Operator Vodafone can likewise analyze phone call patterns in a way that is similar to shopping basket analysis, working out who in a social group may be the most influential. When it comes to contract renewal time, that information can be combined with call volume and profitability data to put a value on a customer and hence influence pricing. An optimal way to price goods and services is according to some, to use analytics and pricing optimization software, combined with real-time input and some human judgment.

Whereas it used to be acceptable to compete on price by investing in efficiency and cost reduction, today, variable pricing implies the ability to alter prices in real time depending on the situation. So information systems have evolved to "slice and dice cost data" (Pitt et al, 2001, p. 53) continuously. This is in an attempt to achieve product differentiation which may be valued by customers but only over "unsustainable" time frames if prices do not enable profitability to be achieved over a longer term. Consequently, strategic finance information may need to feed into the achievement of what may be regarded as "unsustainable" competitive advantage.

Quality

It is often said that many Western organizations in the recent past have tended to regard the provision of enhanced quality as triggering cost increases and that preventative quality measures led to resources having to be incurred before any counter balancing impact from reduced non-conformance costs could be attained. But the lessons learned from Japanese businesses during the 1980's suggested a rejection of the trade-off. In other words, quality failures lead to costs which exceed cost incursions associated with achieving high quality conformance. This argument characterises the view that is espoused in writings concerning quality costing. But there are interrelationships, entailing quality and service provision versus costing issues which have not been effectively addressed.

Quality has many facets. One of these concerns satisfied customers who remain loyal to a company which has built trust through effective quality

of service. The service management literature has over the past few years, suggested that customer loyalty rather than market share drives firm profits (Haskett et al, 1997). In web-enabled firms this has significant implications. Consider, for instance, what internet shoppers go through in making a purchase. The first point of contact for a customer approaching a company website is negotiating navigation of the site. The consumer then advances to
retrieving desired information. Third, some customer support may be sought perhaps in the form of a telephone call, email communication, bulletin board interaction or live chat. Finally, the company's logistics processes put into effect the sales transaction including packaging and shipping, payment processing, guarantee confirmation, and other sales backup service. If the quality of service in the face of the price paid is deemed to be high, loyalty may also result:

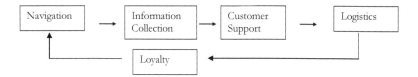

If the navigation and information collection facilities are in place through effective development and investments in technology, this will entice customers to purchase. The variable cost resource requirements to support customers at the pre-purchase stages are usually very low. If logistical problems however occur once an order is placed in terms of, say, product availability, shipment or delivery, extra pressure becomes placed on customer support. This tends to cascade into more extensive logistical resource problems (returns, exchanges, cancellations) and ultimately more extensive cost increases with detrimental competitive consequences. Conversely, if all four aspects of logistical processes are integrated with the requisite information exchange and operational activities, a positive customer experience cycle will result. This will translate into loyalty which has scale effects on per unit navigation and information costs (which are largely fixed) (Hallowell, 2002).

The interdependencies illustrated by this on-line purchasing and organizational processing sequence illustrates the extent to which internal and external failure costs are closely interrelated. Internal failures can be regarded more and more as external failures as the web lends transparency to internal organizational processes in an attempt to be more customer oriented. Quality costs must then adopt a different classification of what is demarcated as conformance and what is seen as non-conformance. In contexts where customers engage in product design, the constitution of prevention costs may be subject to further alterations. In such instances, generalized conceptions of quality costing must give way to more realistic organization-specific understandings of the connections between financial and cost information and quality issues.

Organizational Issues

Aside from managerial concerns, digitised economic activities entail many issues of organizational concern. Traditionally, financial managers have sought to design systems of control which are compatible with the structure of the organization and with the premise upon which organizational activities take place such as the degree of centralization, the riskiness of business unit activities and the culture of the firm. Notionally, it has been assumed that structural contingencies exist between organizational factors and effectiveness and that ultimately, organizational output is dependent on the design and particular practices of financial functions and how they attempt to aid other enterprise management activities. The emergence of web-enabled business operations has altered many of the traditional concepts of organizational relationships and technical contingencies assumed to exist within firms. Balancing organizational controls and processes is now assessed in different terms within many enterprises. The implications for financial management are not negligible and are discussed below.

An important line of research in management has been contingency theory. In the 1960's, some management researchers became interested in the idea that certain organizational forms were more suited to certain structural dimensions than others. Attempts were made to match aspects of the market, the environment, firm size, and technology deployed to organizational form. Some researchers extended this line of thinking to explore whether accounting information systems structures could also be viewed as being more aptly aligned with some organizational dimensions as opposed to others. Although the results of these investigations are seen as being inconclusive (Otley, 1980; Chapman, 1997; Chenhall, 2003), the main thesis that structure is dependent on context along some generic economic continuum still finds appeal in financial management thought. There continues to exist a view that organizational circumstances and contextual variables need to link in to accounting and financial systems configurations.

It might be argued that enterprises operating on digital platforms, or those making extensive use of e-business technologies or simply tracking digitised products and services face a high degree of environmental uncertainty, level of decentralization and degree of organizational interdependence. Consequently, digital enterprises may evidence "a preference for more broad scope, timely, aggregated and integrated information" (Gosselin, 2003). This follows directly from the logic stemming from contingency theory-based arguments that organizations exhibiting such structural variables exhibit an alignment with this form of information. This may be illustrated as follows:

If we consider strategy as an organizational dimension which affects enterprise form, we might categorise a firm as a differentiator based on Porter's framework (1985) or a prospector under Miles and Snow's (1978) typology in terms of the particularity of its product lines or the market it operates in. As noted earlier in this book, Porter (1985) identified different market strategies to enable a competitive advantage to be developed and sustained. Customers may be offered superior value through products or services which are priced lower than the competition for equivalent offerings (cost leadership), or by the provision of unique benefits which exceed the price premium charged to buyers (differentiation). A firm may also choose to adopt a narrow competitive focus within an industry. What is to be avoided is to be "stuck in the middle" (Porter, 1985, p.17) as this leads to an economically unviable situation. Ideally, a firm might seek to become a cost leader whilst also offering a highly differentiated product.

Shoppers often show a preference for private labels beyond the impact of price differentials when compared to established manufacturer brands. Many stores have refined house brands such that they are perceived as being very price competitive and of offering high quality. Such stores include Marks and Spencer in the UK, Germany's Aldi, France's Carrefour, and Wal-Mart in the US. Indeed, the Canadian grocer, Loblaws, which launched the house brand "President's Choice" met with so much success in creating a differentiated cost leader category of products, that the label has itself become a national brand carried by a multitude of other grocers across North America (Boyle, 2003).

If we consider Porter's (1985) taxonomy of business based strategies, firms seeking to design their cost management system and financial controls may do so by adhering to Porter's corporate strategy characteristics. Table 8.1 illustrates the emphasis that may be placed on selected finance function features and corollary strategic emphasis.

Table 8.1: Financial Management Systems and Strategic Emphasis

	Strategic Emphasis	
	Cost Leadership	Product Differentiation
Importance of link between cost and price	Higher	Lower
Relevance of market competitor analysis	Higher	Lower
Importance of standard costs	Higher	Lower
Need for detailed manufacturing performance information	Higher	Lower
Need for detailed R&D design performance information	Lower	Higher

Possibly, one might conclude that since strategy and financial management are increasingly interlinked, all firms should aspire to design jointness of strategic intent and of financial control into to design into their information systems. Finance systems should be customised to fit strategic intent. But if one takes the view that ideally all firms should seek to be product differentiators as well as cost leaders then such convergence of strategy among firms presupposes also convergence of cost management and financial control systems. If strategic excellence implies common appeal to both cost leadership and product differentiation, then supporting financial controls must also become standard across firms. "Best of breed" strategy begets comprehensiveness of financial controls.

Standardizing Financial Management Systems

Some management commentators suggest that the internet makes it difficult to "sustain operational advantages" (Porter, 2001, p.71). Such a view is based on the argument that traditional avenues for differentiating value propositions to consumers through more extensive offerings of product characteristics, differences in customer service provision or variations in packaging, shipping, modes of payment or return policies are eroded by the internet. This is because strategies for differentiating product offerings are readily replicated by competitors and commoditization of products ensues. This then raises the question of how far differentiated strategies are tenable on the internet and of whether linkages and contingencies between contextual factors and management systems design can indeed prevail. One might ask: if differentiated strategies are unsustainable, should enterprises seek to achieve differentiation in the structuring of their information systems and financial management practices?

Other commentators note on the contrary that internet technologies provide firms a source of novel "sustainable operational efficiencies" (Tapscott, 2002, p.7). Commoditization of products and services by competing firms and the standardization of value propositions do not necessarily negate the ability of a firm to differentiate itself. The argument has been made that if the internet, in some contexts, leads to the commoditization of previously differentiated products because of the ease with which it allows comparison-shopping, it also allows the re-differentiation of products by staging customer experiences whether aesthetic, entertainment-based, educational, etc. That is, as products become more standard, organizations appeal to enhanced quality of products to attract customers. They may also offer a greater range of diversifying features and they will invest heavily in branding. But when most organizations within an industry are able to offer high perceived levels of quality, customer service can become the avenue to differentiate its value proposition to the customer. In other words, offering outstanding customer service may become the means for an industry incumbent to keep customers or to draw them away from the competition. Once parity is achieved among competitors in terms of offering excellent customer service, the manner in which the customer experience is staged can become the next step to differentiation. That is, the aesthetics of the buying experience both off line or on line including whether there is excitement or entertainment added to the purchasing process can produce a pathway to attracting customers. Consider, for instance, internet merchants which encourage the customer to make price offers on products and promote haggling, or the level of free on-line entertainment provided on the company's website (Pine and Gilmore, 1999).

But as parity among competitors is reached in this respect, what next? Is there ultimately an increased likelihood of convergence of both product and organizational form in the long run? Moreover, should financial management systems in the long term seek to be standard across firms operating in the same industry if their product offerings and value propositions always indicate a tendency to converge and become commoditized?

In looking back over the past three decades, firms have become more and more alike in their attempts to offer a distinct product. Now that product differentiation is increasingly difficult to achieve, (e.g., how far is a Dell laptop different from an HP laptop?), the focus is toward determining how different organizational arrangements to service the needs of similar customers desiring similar products enable a differentiation angle. In the past, as organizations became more alike, products become more distinct.

Today, as products become more alike, organizations are becoming more unlike. Consider, for instance, Nike versus Adidas in the footwear industry or Zara versus Gap in the garment sector. These firms have widely different organizational arrangements and structures in competing in the same markets. Consider also IBM's Chief Strategist who makes the point as follows: "Just spending money on IT never creates any value. It's what you do differently in terms of business processes that matters" (Bruce Harreld cited in Kirkpatrick, 2003b, p.76).

Possibly, the route to organizational excellence is to seek continuous change in both differentiated value propositions in the face of threats of replication by the competition as well as differentiated internal processes and organizational controls. These trends may be represented as follows:

Traditionally:

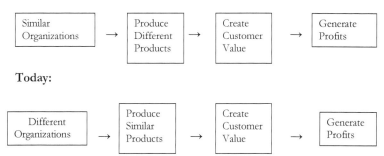

Today:

Attempting to match organizational structure to product market specificity is less and less a plausible strategy for enterprises. This is because organizational specificity has become a means of delivering a standard product. This suggests that financial management systems will continue to be designed with a high degree of organizational customisation. But the implications for financial management systems design are even more extensive. As products become more alike, it is not the end product which becomes the financial focus but the means through which a value proposition to the customer is produced. The routings of organizational processes affect and direct financial management activities. Accounting configurations and standard financial management practices can no longer be guided by common forms producing differentiated products. Rather, differentiated enterprise structurings need to be reflected in the management of firms producing increasingly standard products. Whereas the contingency argument presupposed the existence of ideal organizational forms and therefore of particularity of financial systems which sought to match form to environment, many modern day firms now adopt strategies regarding both products and organizational structuring and technological resources that are deeply intertwined and highly enterprise-specific. It is likely that financial management practices need to adhere to such emerging interdependencies also.

Macro-shifts: Data, Information and Knowledge

At a wider macro- level, many issues affect how financial managers operate within digitised organizations. The manner in which firms create alliances with one another is changing. This is because the economics underpinning value chains which have traditionally been viewed as relevant have altered. In some cases, the structuring of whole industries is being transformed with attendant effects on systems of financial control. Moreover, financial management premises conditioned by conventional notions of trust in business relationships and organizational affairs are undergoing revisions. This further implicates financial management changes.

The costs of using the market to carry out an economic activity has long been regarded as an important determinant of whether firms engage in purchasing from other firms, or whether they internalise the activity. If the costs of carrying out activities in-house are lower than incurring market based prices for having activities undertaken by an outside party, then companies have an incentive to vertically integrate. As Lucking-Reily and Spulber (2001, p.45) note however:

> As market transaction costs fall with the maturation of business-to-business commerce, outsourcing and vertical disintegration will occur resulting in more independent entities along the supply chain.

According to Adler (2002, p.26):

> There is a progressive swelling of the zone between hierarchy and market. Whilst the former relies on the price mechanism and the latter on authority, the "swelling middle" which may adopt a community form that relies on trust.

This trend may lead to value-added communities whereby organizations outsource many non-core functions and make more use of suppliers. They also make greater investments in brand recognition and human capital building and less in physical and working capital (Means and

Schneider, 2000). In such organizations, the ability to manage knowledge, rather than to simply coordinate physical resources gains importance.

From ancient times through to the start of the industrial revolution, power has been associated with ownership of physical resources. The industrial organization has regarded capital and access to it as the principal source of power. But in the closing decades of the twentieth century, information started to be equated with power across different industrial sectors. Some now believe that "future wealth and power will be derived mainly from intangible, intellectual resources: knowledge capital" (Burton-Jones, 1999, p.3). Writers on the emergence and significance of a new economic order based on the management of knowledge assets differentiate data from information and regard both as distinct from knowledge. <u>Data</u> may simply be seen as new numbers and facts. <u>Information</u> is viewed as data interpreted into a meaningful framework. <u>Knowledge</u> becomes information that has been authenticated and thought to be true. Information is consequently processed data and knowledge is information that is made actionable. Boisot (1999, p.12) captures this notion by regarding knowledge as a "property of agents" and information as residing in things that "activates an agent". It is knowledge and its proper management that is viewed as a source of power within enterprises and ultimately as enabling enhanced value creation.

To the extent that financial information relates to quantitative and qualitative signals which are made intelligible to users of the information, a clear role for the finance function is in the collection, aggregation and reporting of such information. In terms of <u>knowledge management</u>, a finance role has to dwell on the build-up of information and the consequent generation of capacities and competencies once the information has been communicated to the information user. At this stage, finance executives capture and relay the qualitative and judgmental essence of raw data and bring this to bear on managerial decisions. If financial management practices are to contribute to knowledge management activities then they must assume an understanding of the components of intellectual capital and the process by which knowledge is created and deployed.

Much research suggests that information transfer is crucial to knowledge management. Effectively, because knowledge production relies on knowledge transfer. If the knowledge production process slows down or stops, then the organization becomes "poorer" since it accumulates experience more slowly (Roberts, 2003). There are different ways of considering knowledge transfers within organizations. Nanaka and Takeuchi (1995) suggest that formal information systems have concentrated on <u>tacit to explicit</u> and <u>explicit to explicit</u> transfers. In effect, some things are not said because if they are to be articulated, a cost must be incurred. Passing from tacit to explicitly codified knowledge comprehensible by others is not costless and often not possible. Information systems can help convert tacit knowledge into explicit knowledge to a degree. More usually they enable explicit to explicit transfers. Financial measures enable different organizational activities to be represented in a standard way. They classify them such that they become economically and managerially actionable. Measures permits the reach of action to be broadened. From data capture to information reporting to knowledge production, key finance capabilities can become implicated. An organization that seeks to formally acknowledge the value of managing its knowledge assets benefits from recognising the finance function as part of that asset base and often regards financial and management accounting practices as principal drivers of knowledge based action.

Transparency in an 'E-world'

The financial control malaise in many firms has been tied to a perceived schism between economic representations of organizational activities and the operational nature of resource flows. Some have pointed to accounting lags, distorted costs and obsolescent financial controls caused by financial professionals having failed to invest in an understanding of organizational realities. For this reason, transparency between resource usage and accounting numbers has been sought by many firms where in accounting information that is reflective of actual resource flows has been missing. In many firms the accountants have been especially concerned to serve the needs of external parties rather than of those of managers and for not recognising the altered logistics of industrial production in their internal accounts. There are firms which see enterprise management as having become more complex without internal financial reporting and cost management practices keeping pace. The changes proposed in financial management debates generated by such concerns have dwelt on how actual resource consumption can be more closely aligned with financial reports of resource consumption. Costing now has to be about physically following the resources and tracking organizational processes. Ultimately, the finance function tries to look at resource flows to make more transparent the links between physical movement and cost accumulation, and to observe and report on the creation of value. It more directly confronts physical production flows to report on their financial consequences.

In digitised organizations where physicality is limited to electron flows and where processes are manifested as instantaneous blips, management approaches resting on physical observability, visual transparency and trust in spatial changes have to be reconsidered. How is the finance function to deal with ephemeral digital transactions each with economic consequences which may be almost negligible but which become very significant with volume? This presents a significant challenge for financial controls. Possibly, a step forward may be not just in the procedures of data capture or in the style of information reporting, but in the skills and abilities of finance professionals to represent information in a new light. For the financial manager to continue to count, it will be increasingly important to show a knowledge of digital products, digital processes and digital consequences using information about enterprise activities as well as those about the competition, the customers and potential customer behaviour that may lead to realised customership.

In contexts where scalability is a relevant economic issue, some important considerations are to be heeded. A decade ago, financial managers deliberated accounting problems that arose where flexible organizational technologies such as computer integrated manufacturing systems were being implemented. But digitized scalable operations have costing implications of a new order. If an investment entails participation in a network that can act locally or globally and where expansion or retrenchment can be adjusted concurrently with changes in the business strategy without altering physical or virtual capacity, then financial management sophistication will need to ratchet up. Important questions of costing, pricing, operational control, planning and performance measurement as well as incentives and rewards are starting to feature in many modern enterprises today. Where a business model relies on driving a very large volume of transactions or keeping up with collectible information about customer and non-customer behaviour, the finance function may need retooling.

Where an organization's architecture alters and adjusts around projects and services it engages in, in conjunction with other networked partners, the underlying accounting activities have to become equally malleable so as to report on differing elements of the dynamic production set up. The possibly high capital costs which enable capacity to be reconfigured around projects or products have to find some basis for being managed. It is widely accepted that habits and premises tend to structure the activities and perceptions of organizational actors and that enterprises are not necessarily the product of deliberate design, but very often reflect the persistence of historical practices. In other words, the justification for everyday practices is taken-for-granted and particular modes of operating and structuring activities are continuously replicated. The legitimacy of particular organizational structures and procedures are then not predicated on constantly reasoned adaptation to constraints and opportunities facing enterprises but because institutionalised customs, professional ideologies and doctrines of effective management prevail unchallenged. This is perhaps one reason why many financial practices like budgeting, variance analysis and overhead cost allocations are carried out in some enterprises where their use could be questioned. The present replicates the past because the past carries a strong element of legitimacy. This is so especially where senior managers support past innovations. Within totally new business models, such tradition has not been a factor and new principles of managing and competing have been developed.

Today many e-businesses and internet "pure plays" adopt organizational structures and managerial procedures that do not conform to traditional modes of operation or structure. Departure from the norm has become the norm in aspects of managerial rationality and there is greater variety and uniqueness of organizational practices. Differentiated enterprise design and the absence of standard control practices are key elements of business competitive strength. The forces of globalization have further fuelled this transition. The lesson may be that managerial adeptness comes from creating the capacity to perceive necessary change. This is never easy but navigating today's complex enterprise environment rests at least in part, on developing the ability to blend strategic and financial enterprise information together with 'big data' to guide managerial action.

BIBLIOGRAPHY

Adler, P.S. (2002) "Markets, Hierarchy and Trust: The Knowledge Economy and the Future of Capitalism" in C.W. Choo and N. Bontis (eds.) *The Strategic Management of Intellectual Capital* (Oxford: Oxford University Press) pp. 23-46.

Anderson, S.W., Hesford, J.W., S. Mark Young (2002) "Factors influencing the performance of ABC teams", *Accounting, Organizations and Society* pp. 195-211.

Argyris, C. and Kaplan, R.S. (1994) "Implementing new knowledge: the case of ABC", *Accounting Horizons* 8 (3) pp. 83-105.

Armstrong, G. (2000) "Information Technology" in *The Financial Management Manual* (London: ABG).

Armstrong, P. (2002) "The costs of activity-based management", *Accounting, Organizations and Society* pp. 99-120.

Atkinson, A., Kaplan,R., Matsumura,E and Young, M. (2007) *Management Accounting* (NJ: Prentice Hall)

Atkinson, J, Hohner, G, Mundt, B, Toxel, R, and Winchel, W. (1991) *Current Trends in Cost Quality*, (Montvale, NJ: NAA).

Balderstone, S and Keef, S. (1999) "Throughout Accounting: Exploding an Urban Myth", *Management Accounting* (October) pp. 26-28.

Bendell,T., Kelly, J., Merry, T. and Sims, F., (1993) *Quality: Measuring and Monitoring*, Century Business.

Bhimani, A. (ed.) (1996) *Management Accounting: European Perspectives*, Oxford: Oxford University Press.

Bhimani, A. (ed) (2003) *Management Accounting in the Digital Economy*, Oxford: Oxford University Press.

Bhimani, A. (2006) *"Management Accounting and Digitalisation"* in A. Bhimani (ed) *Contemporary Issues in Management Accounting* (Oxford University Press).

Bhimani, A. and Bromwich, M. (2001) "Activity Based Costing", *International Encyclopedia of Business and Management* (London: Routledge).

Bhimani, A., Gosselin, M., Ncube, M. and Okano, H. "Activity Based Costing: How Far Have we come Internationally?" *Cost Management*, Vol. 21 (3) pp. 12-17).

Bledsoe, N.L. and Ingram, R.W. (1997) "Customer Satisfaction Through Performance Evaluation", *Journal of Cost Management* (Winter 1997) pp. 43-50. Reprinted with permission. For more information, visit www.wglcorpfinance@riag.com

Boisot, M. (1999) *Knowledge Assets* (Oxford: Oxford University Press).

Borthick, A.F. and Roth, H.P. (1997) "Faster Access to More Information for Better Decisions", *Journal of Cost Management* (Winter) pp. 25-30.

Boyle, M. (2001) "Performance Reviews: Perilous Curves Ahead", *Fortune* (28/5/2001) pp. 103-104.

Boyle, M. (2003), "Brand Killers", *Fortune* (11/8/2003) pp. 50-57.

Bromwich, M. (1990) "The Case for Strategic Management Accounting", *Accounting, Organizations and Society* pp. 231-276.

Bromwich, M. (1991) "Accounting for Strategic Excellence", *Management Accounting and Strategies: New Ideas, New Experiences* (Denmark: SYSTIME).

Bromwich, M. and Bhimani, A. (1994) *Management Accounting: Pathways to Progress*, London; CIMA.

Bryan, L and Joyce, C. (2007) "Better strategy through organzational designs" *The McKinsey Quarterly* (2)pp.21-29.

Budhwani, K. (2001) "Jack be Nimble", *CMA Management* (Sept.) pp. 22-25.

Burton-Jones, A. (1999) *Knowledge Capitalism* (Oxford: Oxford University Press).

Buzzell, R. and Gale, B. (1987) *The PIMS Principles: Linking Strategy to Performance* (New York: The Free Press).

Carr, L.P. (1995) "Cost of Quality – Making it Work", *Journal of Cost Management* (Spring) pp. 61-65.

Chalos, P. and Poon, M. (2001) "Participative Budgeting and Performance: A State of the Art Review and Re-Analysis", *Advances in Management Accounting*, Vol.10, pp. 171-202.

Chartered Institute of Management Accountants (2000) *Management Accounting Official Terminology* (London: CIMA).

CIMA *Performance Management in the Manufacturing Sector*, 1993.

CIMA Technical Briefing (2002) *Latest Trends in Corporate Performance Measurement*, (July).

CMA Canada (1999) "Management Accounting Guideline", *Financial Risk Management*.

Cheatham, C.B. and Cheatham, L.R. (1996) "Redesigning Cost Systems: Is Standard Costing Obsolete?" *Accounting Horizons* (December) pp. 23-31.

Chenhall, RH. (2003) "Management Control Systems Design within its Organizational Context: Findings from Contingency-based Research and Directions for the Future", *Accounting, Organizations and Society* (28), pp. 127-168.

Cooper, G. (1992) *Strategic Business Information*, Paper presented at the LSE MARG Conference (2 April).

Cooper, R. (1989) "You Need a New Costing System When…", *Harvard Business Review* (February).

Cooper, R. (1996) "Activity Based Costing and the Lean Enterprise" in *Journal of Cost Management* (Winter) pp. 6-14. Reprinted with permission. For more information, visit http://www.wglcorpfinance@riag.com/

Corboy, M. and O'Corrbui, D. (1999) "The Seven Deadly Sins of Strategy", *Management Accounting* (UK) (November) pp. 29-30.

Cravens, S.K. and Guilding, C. (2001) "An Empirical Application Study of Strategic Management Accounting Techniques", *Advances in Management Accounting* pp. 95-124.

Dale, B.G. and Plunkett, J.J. (1999) *Quality Costing* (London: Gower).

Davenport, T. (2006) "Competing on Analytics" *Harvard Business Review* pp. 36-44.

Davenport, T. (2000) *Mission Critical – Realizing the Promise of Enteprise Systems* (Boston: Harvard Business School Press).

Davenport, T. (2010) *Analytics at Work: Smarter Decisions, Better Results* (Boston: Harvard Business School Press).

Dedera, C.R. (1996) "Harris Semiconductor ABC: World-wide Implementation and Total Integration", *Journal of Cost Management* (Spring) pp. 44-58. Reprinted with permission. For more information, visit http://www.wglcorpfinance@riag.com/

Dent, J. (1990) "Strategy, Organization and Control: Some Possibilities for Accounting Research", *Accounting, Organizations and Society* pp. 3-25.

Develin, N and Bellis-Jones, R. (1999) *No Customer – No Business: The True Value of Activity Based Cost Management* (London: ABG).

Drtina, R.E. and Monetti, G.A. (1995) "Controlling Flexible Business Strategies", *Journal of Cost Management* (Fall) pp. 42-49. Reprinted with permission. For more information, visit http://www.wglcorpfinance@riag.com/

Drury, C. (1999) "Standard Costing: A Technique at Variance with Modern Management" *Management Accounting* pp. 56-58.

Dutton, J.J. and Ferguson, M. (1996) "Target Costing at Texas Instrument", *Journal of Cost Management* (Fall) pp. 33-38. Reprinted with permission. For more information, visit http://www.wglcorpfinance@riag.com/

Dye, B. (2002) *Strategic Direction* (Fall).

Eklund, B. (2000) "Presence of Mind: Industrial Robotos are Smarter and Cheaper than Ever" *Red Herring* (August) pp. 258-262.

Epstein, M. (2000) "Customer Profitability Analysis" *Management Accounting Guideline* (Canada: SMAC).

Estrin, T. and Kantor, J. (1998) "Accounting for Throughout Time", *Advances in Management Accounting* Vol 6 pp. 55-74.

Evans, J.R. and Lindsay, W.M. (2001) *Management and the Control of Quality* (NY: West Wadsworth).

Fargher, N. and Morse, D. (1998) "Quality Costing: Planning the Trade Off", *Journal of Cost Management* (Jan/Feb) pp.14-22.

Fisher, J. (1995) "Implementing Target Costing", *Journal of Cost Management* (Summer) pp. 50-59. Reprinted with permission. For more information, visit http://www.wglcorpfinance@riag.com/

Foster, G. (1996) "Management Accounting in 2000", *Journal of Cost Management* (Winter) pp. 36-39. Reprinted with permission. For more information, visit http://www.wglcorpfinance@riag.com/

Foster, G., Gupta, M and Sjoblom, L (1996) "Customer Profitability Analysis: Challenges and New Directions", *Journal of Cost Management* (Spring 1996) pp. 5-17.

Francis, G. and Minchington, C. (2000) "Value based Management in Practice", *Management Accounting* (February) pp. 46-47.

Gardiner, M. (1997) "Financial Ratios: Can you trust them?" *Management Accounting* (September) p.30.

Gates, S. and Kulik, T. (1999) "Aligning incentive performance measures and incentives in European companies" (Conference Board Research Report) (www.conference-board.org/products/research.cfm).

Ghemawat, P. (2011) World 3.0: Global Prosperity and How to Achieve It (Boston, Mass.: HBSP)

Goldratt, E.M. (1990) *The Haystack Syndrome: Sifting Information Out of the Data Ocean* (Croton-on-Hudson, NY: North River Press).

Goldratt, E.M. and Cox, J. (1984) *The Goal*, (London: Gower).

Gosselin, M. (1997) "The Effect of Strategy and Organizational Structure on the Adoption and Implementation of Activity Based Costing", *Accounting, Organizations and Society* pp. 105-122.

Granlund, M. and Malmi, T. (2002) "Moderate Impact of ERPS on Management Accounting: A Lay or Permanent Outcome" *Management Accounting Research* pp. 299-321.

Guilding, C. Cravens, K.S. and Tayles, M. (2000) "An International Comparison of Strategic Management Accounting Practices", *Management Accounting Research* pp. 113-135.

Hallowell, R. (2002), *Service on the Internet: The Effects of Physical Service on Scalability* Harvard Business School Note 5-802-168.

Hamel, G. (1996) "Strategy as Revolution", *Harvard Business Review* (July/August) pp. 69-82.

Hamel, G. and Prahalad, C.K. (1994) "Competing for the future", *Harvard Business Review* (July/August) pp. 122-128.

Handy, C. (1998) *The Age of Unreason* (London: Arrow).

Holmen, J.S. (1995) "ABC vs TOC: It's a matter of time", *Management Accounting* (US) (January) pp. 37-40.

Hopwood, A. G. (2000) "Costs Count in the Strategic Agenda" *FT Mastering Management* (6 November), pp. 8-10.

Hunton, J.E. McEwen, R.A. and Wier, B. (2002) "The Reaction of Financial Analysts to ERP Implementation Plans" *Journal of Information Systems* pp. 242-257.

Innes,J, Mitchell, F. and Sinclair, D. (2000) "A Tale of Two Surveys", *CIMA Research Update* (Spring/Summer) p.4.

Johnson, HT, (1995) "Management Accounting in the 21st Century", *Journal of Cost Management* (Fall) pp. 15-20.

Juras, P. and Dierks, P (1993) "Blue Ridge", *Management Accounting* (Dec) pp. 57-59.

Kaplan, R.S. (1995) "New Roles for Management Accountants", *Journal of Cost Management* (Fall) pp. 6-14. Reprinted with permission. For more information, visit http://www.wglcorpfinance@riag.com/

Kaplan, R.S. and Cooper, R. (1998) *Cost and Effect: Using Integrated Cost Systems to Drive Profitability and Performance* (Boston, Massachusetts: HBS Press).

Kaplan, R.S. and Norton, D.P. (1996) *The Balanced Scorecard* (Boston, Massachusetts: HBS Press).

Kaplan, R.S. and Norton, D.P. (2001) *The Strategy Focused Organization: How Balanced Scorecard Companies Thrive in the New Business Environment* (Boston, Mass: HBSP).

Kato, Y., Böer, G. and Chow, C.W. (1995) "Target Costing: an Integrative Management Process", *Journal of Cost Management* (Spring) pp. 39-51. Reprinted with permission. For more information, visit www.wglcorpfinance@riag.com

Kelly, K. (1998) *New Rules for the New Economy* (New York: Viking).

King, A.M. (1997), "Three Significant Digits", *Journal of Cost Management* (Winter) pp. 31-37. Reprinted with permission. For more information, visit www.wglcorpfinance@riag.com

Kirkpatrick, D. (2003a) "How to Erase the Middleman in one Easy Lesson", *Fortune* (17 March) p.76.

Kirkpatrick, D. (2003b) "Tech: Where the Action Is", *Fortune* (12 May) pp. 24-29.

Koch,C. (2003) "The ABCs of ERP", *Accounting Education News* (Summer) pp. 7-10.

Lapré, A. and Van Wassenhove, N.L. (2002) "Learning across Lines: The Secret to More Efficient Factories" *Harvard Business Review* (Oct) pp. 107-111.

Luck, V. (1994) "Made to Measure", *Accountancy Age* 1994.

Lynch, D. (1999) "Focus on Quality", *Management Accounting* (September) pp.30-31.

Lynch, R. (2000) *Corporate Strategy* (FT/Prentice Hall).

MacArthur, J.B. (1996) "Performance Measures that count: monitoring variables of strategic importance", *Journal of Cost Management* (Fall) pp. 39-45. Reprinted with permission. For more information, visit www.wglcorpfinance@riag.com

Malmi, T. (1999) "Activity-based costing diffusion across organizations: an exploratory empirical analysis of Finnish firms", *Accounting, Organizations and Society* pp. 649-672.

Means, D. and Schneider, D. (2000) *Meta-capitalism: The E-Business Revolution and the Design of the 21st Century Companies and Markets* (NY: John Wiley).

McCann, M. (2000) "Turning Vision into Reality", *Management Accounting* (January) pp. 36-37.

McCunn, P. (1998) "The Balanced Scorecard… The Eleventh Commandment", *Management Accounting*, (December) pp 34-36.

McNair, C.J. (1996) "To serve the Customer Within" in *Journal of Cost Management* (winter) pp. 40-43. Reprinted with permission. For more information, visit www.wglcorpfinance@riag.com

McNair, C.J. (1997) "The New Finance: Shaping Functional Relevance for the New Millennium", *CMA Magazine* (February) pp. 11-14.

Mayor, M. (2007) "Activity Based Costing and Management: A Critical Review" in Hopper et al.

Maynard, M. (2001) "Tyremaking technology is on a roll", *Fortune* 28.5.2001, pp. 85-89.

Mintzberg, H., Quinn, J. and Goshal, S. (1999) *The Strategy Process* (Hemel Hampstead: Pearson).

Mintzberg, H. (1978) "Patterns in Strategy Formulation", *Management Science* pp. 934-948.

Moore, G. (2002)" How Intel took Moore's Law From Idea to Ideology Interview", *Fortune* (11 Nov.), p.42.

Morrow, M. (1992) *Activity Based Management* (London: Woodhead-Faulkner).

Musgrove, C.L. and Fox, M.J. (1991) *Quality Costs: Their Impact on Company Strategy and Profitability* (Herts; UK: Technical Communications Ltd).

Nagumo, T. and Donlon, B. (2006) "Integrating the balanced scorecard and COSO ERM frameworks" *Cost Management* (July/August) pp. 20-30.

Naylor, J. (1999) *Management* (London: Financial Times Pitman).

Nicolaou, A.I. (2001) "Interactive Effects of Strategic and Cost Management Systems on Managerial Performance", *Advances in Management Accounting* (Vol.10) pp. 203-226.

Nonaka, I. And Takenchi, H. (1995) *The Knowledge Creating Company: How Japanese Companies Create the Dynamics of Innovation*, (Oxford: Oxford University Press).

Noreen, S., Smith, D. and Mackey, J.T. (1995) *The Theory of Constraints and its Implementation for Management Accounting* (Montrale, New Jersey: IMA).

Nyamori, R.O., Perera, M. and Lawrence, S. (2001) "The Concept of Strategic Change for Management Accounting Research", *Journal of Accounting Literature* pp. 62-83.

O'Leary, G. (2002) "Knowledge of Management across the Enterprise Resource Planning Life Cycle", *International Journal of Accounting Information Systems* pp. 99-110.

Otley, D. (2001) "Extending the boundaries of management accounting research: Developing systems for performance management", *Management Accounting Research* pp. 243-261.

Palmer, R.J. (1992) "Strategic Goals and Objectives and the Design of Strategic Management Accounting Systems" <u>Advances in Management Accounting</u> pp. 179-204.

Peters, T. (1985) In Pursuit of Excellence.

Piercy, N.F. (1999) "Strategic Management: Strategizing your way to the future", B*usiness Digest* (June) pp 1-42.

Player, R.S. and Keys, D.E. (1995a) "Lessons from the ABM Battlefield: Getting off to the Right Start", *Journal of Cost Management* (Spring) pp. 26-37. Reprinted with permission. For more information, visit http://www.wglcorpfinance@riag.com/

Player, R.S. and Keys, D.E. (1995b), "Lessons from the ABM Battlefield: Developing the Pilot", *Journal of Cost Management* (Summer) pp. 20-34. Reprinted with permission. For more information, visit http://www.wglcorpfinance@riag.com/

Player, R.S. and Keys, D.E. (1995c) "Lessons from the ABM Battlefield: Moving from Pilot to Mainstream", *Journal of Cost Management* (Fall) pp. 31-41. Reprinted with permission. For more information, visit http://www.wglcorpfinance@riag.com/

Porter, M (1998) *Competitive Advantage* (NY: Free Press).

Porter, M (1998) *Competitive Strategy* (London: Simon and Shuster).

Porter, M.E. (1999) quoted in Surowiecki, J. "The return of Michael Porter", *Fortune*, February 1, pp 135-138.

Poston, R. and Grabski, S. (2001) "Financial Impacts of ERP Implementation", *International Journal of Accounting Information Systems* pp. 271-254.

Prahalad, C.K. and Hamel, G. (1990) "The Core Competence of the Corporation", *Harvard Business Review*, Vol 68 No 3, pp 79-91.

Pryor, T. (1997) "Making New Things Familiar and Familiar Things New", *Journal of Cost Management* (Winter) pp. 38-42. Reprinted with permission. For more information, visit http://www.wglcorpfinance@riag.com/

Pryor, T. and Sahm, J. (1995) *Using Activity Based Management for Continuous Improvement: A step by step Approach* (Arlington, Texas: ICMS).

Radharkrishnan, S. and Srinidhi, B. (1997) "Avoiding the Death Spiral: A Case for Activity Based Costing", *Journal of Cost Management* pp 19-24. Reprinted with permission. For more information, visit http://www.wglcorpfinance@riag.com/

Ray, M. (1995) "Cost Management for Product Development", *Journal of Cost Management* (Spring) pp. 52-60. Reprinted with permission. For more information, visit http://www.wglcorpfinance@riag.com/

Rayport, J.F. and Jaworski, B.J. (2002) *E-Commerce* (Boston, MA: McGraw Hill).

Reeve, J.M. (1996) "Projects, Models, and Systems - Where is ABM headed?", *Journal of Cost Management* (Summer), pp. 5-16. Reprinted with permission. For more information, visit http://www.wglcorpfinance@riag.com/

Rigelsford, K. and Sharp, I. (2000) "Accounting for the new Economy", *Accountancy* (May) pp 124-125.

Roberts, H. (2003) "Management Accounting and the Knowledge Production Process" in A. Bhimani (ed.) *Management Accounting in the Digital Economy* (Oxford: Oxford University Press).

Roberts, M.W. and Silvester, K.J (1996) "Why ABC Failed and how it May Yet Succeed", *Journal of Cost Management* (Winter) pp. 23-35. Reprinted with permission. For more information, visit http://www.wglcorpfinance@riag.com/

Roslender, R., Hart, S. and Ghosh, J. (1998) "Strategic Management Accounting: Refocusing the Agenda", *Management Accounting* (UK) (Dec) pp 44-46.

Rousseau, Y. and Rousseau, P. (2000) "Common Pitfalls of the Balanced Scorecard", *CMA Management* (December/January) pp 26-29.

Ruhl, J.M. (1996) "An introduction to the Theory of Constraints", *Journal of Cost Management* pp 43-48. Reprinted with permission. For more information, visit http://www.wglcorpfinance@riag.com/

Ruhl, J.M. (1996) "Activity Based Management. Lessons from the ABM Battlefield and World Class Manufacturing; The Next Decade", *Journal of Cost Management* (Spring) pp. 26-37. Reprinted with permission. For more information, visit http://www.wglcorpfinance@riag.com/

Salover, G. and Spence, A.M. (2002) *Creating and Capturing Value* (New York: John Wiley).

Sandoe, K. Corbitt, G. and Boykin, R. (2001) *Enterprise Integration* (NY: Wiley).

Scapens, R., Jazayeri, M. (2003) "ERP Systems and Management Accounting Changes: Opportunities or Impacts?" *European Accounting Review* pp. 201-233.

Scapens, R., Jazayeri, M and Scapens, J. (1998) "SAP: Integrated Information Systems and the Implications for Management Accountants", *Management Accounting* (September) pp 46-48.

Scapens, R.W. and Roberts, J. (1993), "Accounting and Control: A Case Study of Resistance to Accounting Change", *Management Accounting Research*, pp. 1-32.

Schlender, B. (2002) "Intel's $10 Billion Gamble", Fortune (11 Nov.) pp. 36-41).

Shanahan, Y.P. (1995) "Implementing an ABC System - Lessons from the Australian Post", *Journal of Cost Management* (Summer) pp. 60-64. Reprinted with permission. For more information, visit http://www.wglcorpfinance@riag.com/

Shank, J.K. (1996) "New Wines in Old battles: Reichard Maschinen GmbH", *Journal of Cost Management* (summer) pp 49-59. Reprinted with permission. For more information, visit http://www.wglcorpfinance@riag.com/

Shank, J. and Govindarajan, V. (1996) *Strategic Cost Analysis* (Irwin).

Sheridan, T (1998) "The Changing Shape of the Finance Function", *Management Accounting* pp 18-20.

Shields, M.D. and McEwens, M.A. (1996) "Implementing ABC Systems Successfully" in *Journal of Cost Management* (Winter) pp. 15-23. Reprinted with permission. For more information, visit http://www.wglcorpfinance@riag.com/

Simmonds, K. (1988) "Strategic Management Accounting" in Cowe, R. (ed) *Handbook of Management Accounting* (London: Gower) pp. 26-29.

Simons, R. (2000) *Performance Measurement and Control Systems for Implementing Strategy* (Boston, Massachusetts: HBS Press).

Slywotzky, A.J. (2000) "The Age of the Choiceboard" *Harvard Business Review* (Jan/Feb.) pp.4/5.

Smith, K. and Leksan, M. (1991) "A Manufacturing Case Study on Activity Based Costing" *Journal of Cost Management* (Summer). Reprinted with permission. For more information, visit http://www.wglcorpfinance@riag.com/

Smith, M (1999) "Realising the benefits from Investment in ERP" *Management Accounting* (November) p.34.

Tapscott, D. (2002), *Rethinking Strategy in a Networked World* <u>Strategy and Business</u> pp.2-8.

Wilson, R. and Chua, W.F. (1993) *Managerial Accounting: Method and Meaning* (London: Chapman and Hall).

Winterton, J. (2000) "Stirred by the Genius of the Net", *The Industry Standard Europe* (9.11.2000) pp. 77-79.

Wisner, P.S. (2001) "The Impact of Work Teams on Performance: A quasi-experimental field study", *Advances in Management Accounting* (Vol.10) pp. 1-28.